THE GOSPEL

according to

GRACE

THE GOSPEL ACCORDING TO GRACE

A CLEAR COMMENTARY ON
THE BOOK OF ROMANS

by Pastor Chuck Smith

THE WORD FOR TODAY
Box 8000 Costa Mesa CA 92628

THE BOOK OF ROMANS

Note To The Reader

The Gospel According To Grace is a general, introductory commentary on the book of Romans, the Apostle Paul's magnificent statement of Christian truths. Based on bible studies delivered at Calvary Chapel of Costa Mesa by Pastor Chuck Smith, it is written for the average layman. Pastor Chuck explains these truths of God in a clear and understandable manner.

Should you desire to study the book of Romans in greater depth, we reccomend the in depth cassette tape set on the book of Romans available through THE WORD FOR TODAY.

———————

Quotes from the book of Romans are printed in **bold face type.** These quotes are followed by references to Chapter & Verse. eg. (1:10) Sometimes the letters "a,b, or c" are used in these references to indicate a partial quote of the verse.

Unless otherwise specified, the King James Version is used for all scriptural quotes. Translational references and occasional paraphrases are used by the author to amplify or clarify certain passages.

CHAPTER 1
THE LOST WORLD

The Book of Romans begins, **Paul, a servant of Jesus Christ** (1:1a). The word "servant" in Greek is *doulos*, which means "bond-slave." A bond-slave had no rights of his own. He belonged totally to his master. As a bond-slave of Jesus Christ, Paul was living totally for his Master.

Paul was **called to be an apostle** (1:1b). "Apostle" literally means "one who is sent." In his calling Paul was **separated unto the gospel of God** (1:1c). We remember that in the Book of Acts the Holy Spirit said, "Separate me Barnabas and Saul [Paul] for the work whereunto I have called them. And when they had fasted and prayed, and laid their hands on them, they sent them away" (Acts 13:2-3). Paul was sent by the Holy Spirit to bear the Gospel to the Gentiles. The word "gospel" means "good news." To hear some people tell it, God is bad news. But that's not true! God's love for us in Jesus Christ is *good news*.

(Which he had promised afore by his prophets in the holy scriptures) (1:2). This Gospel wasn't an event that simply happened without warning. The message of the Gospel, especially to the Gentiles, was spoken of by God through the prophets. (When Paul refers to the "holy scriptures," he has only the Old Testament in mind.)

The good news is about God's Son, **Jesus Christ our Lord** (1:3a). So often we read the "Lord Jesus Christ" and think of this as His first, middle, and last name. "Lord" is not His name; it is His title. The Greek word for "lord" is kurios.

"Jesus" is His name. This is a Greek translation of the Hebrew name "Joshua," meaning "Jehovah is salvation." In Matthew's gospel we read, "The angel of the Lord appeared unto him in a dream, saying, Joseph, thou son of David, fear not to take unto thee Mary thy wife: for that which is conceived in her is of the Holy Ghost. And she shall bring forth a son, and thou shalt call his name Jesus: for he shall save his people from their sins" (Matthew 1:20-21). His name implies His mission: "he shall save his people from their sins." "Christ" is Greek for the Hebrew word meaning "messiah" or "the anointed one of God," the one whom God had promised to send to His people. "Christ" or "Messiah" signifies His ministry as the fulfillment of the promise of God. "Jesus Christ our Lord" signifies the believer's relationship to Him.

In the Bible we read, "If thou shalt confess with thy mouth the Lord Jesus, and shalt believe in thine heart that God hath raised him from the dead, thou shalt be saved. For with the heart man believeth unto righteousness; and with the mouth confession is made unto salvation" (Romans 10:9-10). The first part of that passage would be better translated, "If thou shalt confess with thy mouth that Jesus Christ is Lord." Our obligation is more than confessing belief in Jesus Christ. You can believe that Jesus Christ is the Son of God, but not be saved. You can believe that He died on the cross for your sins, yet not be born again. It's necessary to submit your life to Him as *Lord* of your life in order to have salvation.

Concerning his Son Jesus Christ our Lord, which was made of the seed of David according to the

flesh (1:3). As king of Israel, David had a beautiful house in Jerusalem. When he saw the tent where people were worshiping God, he said, "Here I am dwelling in this exquisite palace, and all we have is a tent for God. I'm going to build a beautiful house for Him."

The prophet Nathan told him, "David, that sounds like a marvelous idea." But that night the Lord spoke to Nathan and told him that he had spoken hastily. "Go back and tell David that he can't build My house. It's good that the desire is in his heart, but he has shed too much blood." To soften David's disappointment God told Nathan, "Tell David that I'm going to build him a house."

So, the prophet told David, "I have some good news and some bad news. The bad news is that you can't build a house for God. The good news is that God is going to build you a house." God was telling David that through him the Messiah would come. God would establish His kingdom through David's seed, and there would never lack one from his offspring to sit upon the throne.

David was overwhelmed. "Who am I, O Lord God, and what is mine house, that thou hast brought me hitherto?" (I Chronicles 17:1-16). The Lord took David from following after sheep and made him ruler over His people. Now He planned to build David a house and establish his throne forever.

"Lord, what can I say?" David was speechless. Now that's a remarkable statement for David to make, because he was very gifted with words. Whenever I find it difficult to express my feelings to God, I turn to the Psalms where David expresses such things so well. Yet, here David was speechless because of God's goodness and grace. It's a wonderful experience when God so blesses us that words become inadequate to describe our feelings. As Savonarola said, "When prayer reaches its ultimate, words are impossible."

As we trace the genealogy of Christ back through Mary in Luke's gospel, we find Him coming through the line of David. Jesus is God incarnate and the seed of David, the beautiful God-Man, **declared to be the Son of God with power, according to the spirit of holiness** (1:4), for He was conceived by the Holy Spirit.

Some people say that the Virgin Birth is only mentioned in two of the Gospels and so we don't need to accept the event as fact. If we don't accept the Virgin Birth as fact, then who was Jesus' father? How many times does God have to tell us something before we believe it? God has told us twice. Isn't that enough? Jesus *is* **the seed of David according to the flesh; and declared to be the Son of God with power, according to the spirit of holiness, by the resurrection from the dead** (1:3b-4).

By whom we have received grace and apostleship, for obedience to the faith among all nations, for his name (1:5). Paul had the anointing and calling of an apostle, although he considered himself to be the chief of sinners (I Timothy 1:12-15).

Among whom are ye also the called of Jesus Christ. And now a salutation, **To all that be in Rome, beloved of God, called to be saints: Grace to you and peace from God our Father, and the Lord Jesus Christ** (1:6-7). The first title given to the believers, "beloved of God," fits everyone. It's often difficult for us to accept God's love, perhaps because sometimes we don't really love ourselves. If we don't love ourselves, we wonder how can God love us. But He does!

More than that, we're called "saints." It was tragic when the Church decided to honor certain people for special deeds, thus setting criteria for sainthood. If a miracle occurred by praying to a deceased person who was known for doing outstanding works during his life-

time, then the Church chose to consider that person a
saint. But don't worry if the Church overlooked you. God
has chosen you, and it's better to be considered a saint by
God than from the Church any day. You have been called
a saint. Now live up to your calling.

**Grace to you and peace from God our Father,
and the Lord Jesus Christ** (1:7b). Grace and peace are
called the Siamese Twins of the New Testament because
they're always coupled together. This is the proper order
of the two words; you can't have the *peace* of God until
you've first experienced His grace.

Peace *with* God is necessary before you can have the
peace *of* God. They're two different experiences. You can
experience peace with God when you're saved, and still
not know the peace of God.

Many Christians are upset, worried, and frantic.
They're not sure that God will work everything out, and
their lives are in turmoil. They don't have the peace *of*
God. This is the peace to which Paul is referring. After I
recognize that the grace of God is *unmerited* favor, I can
experience the peace of God because I'm no longer striving. I realize that His blessings haven't been earned by
my merit or goodness. I'm now trusting in God's completed work, and I'm at peace in my relationship with
God. I've totally committed myself to Him.

First, said Paul, **I thank my God through Jesus
Christ for you all** (1:8a). In the New Testament we're
taught to pray to God through Jesus Christ. "Whatsoever
ye shall ask in my name," Jesus said, "that will I do, that
the Father may be glorified in the Son. If you shall ask
any thing in my name, I will do it" (John 14:13-14).

**Your faith is spoken of throughout the whole
world** (1:8b). The godly faith of the Roman believers was
well known throughout the Church world.

For God is my witness, whom I serve with my spirit in the gospel of his Son, that without ceasing I make mention of you always in my prayers (1:9). Paul's prayers were in the closet, so to speak. Paul states, "God is my witness," because he can't call on any man to verify his prayers. He was following the instructions Jesus gave us when He said, "Enter into thy closet, and when thou hast shut thy door, pray to thy Father which is in secret" (Matthew 6:6a).

Making request, if by any means now at length I might have a prosperous journey by the will of God to come unto you. For I long to see you, that I may impart unto you some spiritual gift, to the end ye may be established (1:10-11). Paul's motive for going to Rome wasn't to see the great Forum or the Circus Maximus, but to minister to the believers. He wanted to impart some spiritual gift through which they might be strengthened.

That is, that I may be comforted together with you by the mutual faith both of you and me (1:12). Gathering together with God's people has a two-way effect. You cannot minister to others without being ministered to yourself. That's the beauty of sharing our spiritual gifts with one another. Jesus said, "Give, and it shall be given unto you" (Luke 6:38a). Sowing the truth in love always reaps the same.

Now I would not have you ignorant, brethren, that oftentimes I purposed to come unto you, (but was let hitherto) that I might have some fruit among you also, even as among other Gentiles (1:13). Paul wanted to visit them before, but had been hindered. The apostle wasn't deliberately slighting the Romans by his absence.

I am debtor both to the Greeks, and to the Barbarians; both to the wise, and to the unwise (1:14).

"Barbarian" is an unfortunate word here because its modern meaning is "savage". The term originated with the Greeks who thought all foreign languages sounded like "bar-bar" on incomprehensible babbling. The expression actually meant anyone who didn't speak Greek. It wasn't a derogatory expression in Paul's day.

So, as much as in me is, I am ready to preach the gospel to you that are at Rome also. For I am not ashamed of the gospel of Christ: for it is the power of God unto salvation to everyone that believeth; to the Jew first, and also to the Greek (1:15-16). Jesus Christ is God's power of salvation. To whom? To everyone who believes.

For therein is the righteousness of God revealed from faith to faith: as it is written, The just shall live by faith (1:17). Paul begins early in the book to introduce the two themes of his message: (1) the righteousness which is of God through faith and (2) the just shall live by faith. Man's righteousness before God isn't predicated upon the Law of Moses or the works of man, but upon believing in the work of God.

For the wrath of God is revealed from heaven against all ungodliness and unrighteousness of men, who hold the truth in unrighteousness (1:18). Verse 16 emphasizes the *power* of God, verse 17 the *righteousness* of God, and verse 18 the *wrath* of God. People talk about the power and righteousness of God, but they often deny or ignore one aspect of God's nature—His wrath.

The Mosaic Law was written on two tablets of stone. The first tablet dealt with man's relationship with God; the second dealt with man's relationship with his fellow man. A man is ungodly when he isn't right with God; he is also unrighteous when he isn't right with his fellow man as God wishes him to be.

The wrath of God is to be revealed against the ungodliness and unrighteousness of men. The two tablets of stone are thus tied together. You cannot have a right relationship with God and a wrong relationship with your brother. If you say that you love God, then you have to love your brother also. You cannot love God and hate your brother.

Some people hold the truth of God, but they hold it in unrighteousness. You say you believe in God. Well that's wonderful. It's the right place to start, but alone it isn't enough. The devils believe in God, so what makes you different from them? You must believe in God *and* trust in His salvation. That's the difference!

Because that which may be known of God is manifest in them; for God hath shewed it unto them. For the invisible things of him from the creation of the world are clearly seen, being understood by the things that are made, even his eternal power and Godhead; so that they are without excuse (1:19-20). The existence of God is universally attested to. The design of His work is self-evident to all. Those who deny or ignore God are totally without excuse.

When they knew God, they glorified him not as God (1:21a). Paul's first indictment against natural men is that knowing God, but they didn't glorify Him as God.

How many times I have failed to honor God and instead found myself arguing with Him. Peter and Paul argued with the Lord. This trait is part of my human weakness, and it doesn't give glory to God. By arguing with God, I bring Him down to my level, and even reduce Him below my level, because my premise is that I'm right and He isn't. It's ridiculous! God knows far more about my own situation than I do.

Neither were [they] thankful (1:21b). I Thessalonians 5:18 says, "In everything give thanks: for this is the will of God in Christ Jesus concerning you." The circumstances of your life have been ordained by God and are working together according to a divine plan. "The steps of a good man are ordered by the Lord" (Psalm 37:23a). Nothing happens to you by accident. Don't say, "Good luck!" There is no such thing for a Christian. Similarly whenever you complain about your circumstances you're actually complaining about God. He has brought certain situations into your life for the best. When you moan and groan, God is displeased with your unthankful heart.

As Christians we need to learn to accept the things that come across our paths. "We know that all things work together for good to them that love God" (Romans 8:28a). May this truth be embedded in our hearts! When events that seem like tremendous tragedies come, we often ask, "If God loves me how could He allow this to happen?" We can't understand everything that comes across our paths, and God doesn't promise us total understanding. The lyrics to an old southern song have brought comfort to many.

> Further along we'll know all about it.
> Further along we'll understand why.
> Cheer up, my brother, live in the sunshine.
> We'll understand it all by and by.

The point of the song is that in heaven we can sit down with Jesus and ask, "Why did that have to happen?" Actually, when we get to heaven, we'll be so excited and full of rejoicing that we'll just enjoy it all! God doesn't owe us any explanations; we owe Him our complete obedience, surrender, and submission.

Imagine the potter with the clay. In front of him is the potter's wheel used to shape the vessel. After getting the clay to the right consistency, he throws it on the center of the wheel and begins to form it. The clay leaps up at his touch as he works it.

Now as clay in the hands of the potter, so am I in the hands of God. The wheel on which the potter molds the clay is like the circumstances of my life. The wheel is under the total control of the potter, and that's all the clay needs to know. "It hurts!" the clay may complain. "I wonder how much longer the potter will mold me. Won't he ever stop?"

God molds me by ordaining the circumstances of my life. I submit to Him so that He might work in me His eternal purposes. "I thank You, God, for all the disappointments and losses that I have experienced." Paul says, "The sufferings of this present time are not worthy to be compared with the glory which shall be revealed in us" (Romans 8:18). "For our light affliction, which is but for a moment, worketh for us a far more exceeding and eternal weight of glory" (2 Corinthians 4:17).

God's work in your life may be painful right now, but He's aiming at the eternal goal. He wants to bring you into a more glorious entrance into His kingdom. Maybe He has to deprive you now of something that you feel is so very important, but He overlooks your temporary ease for your eternal interest. He has such wonderful things prepared, and He's trying to lead us toward them. If only we would learn to flow with the Spirit and be thankful in all things, because we belong to God. If we live this way we'll never be disappointed.

Accepting God's will for your life is like the little boy who built a model ship. He carefully glued into place all the masts, riggings, and sails. After months of labor he took it down to the pond and gently laid it on the water. Proudly, he watched as the wind filled the sails and the little boat sailed gracefully across the pond. Midway across the lake a strong gust of wind knocked the sailboat over and it sank. The little boy looked up and said, "Wow! What a great wind for flying a kite!" When God stops you on one venture, be open to what He may have in mind. Don't sit down and cry. He has something else for you to do. Look for it!

God often has to deal with us severely, because we're not open and listening to Him. We easily get into ruts with our well-ordered lives and stop looking for what God wants us to have. Perhaps you're at a good job, getting seniority, and doing fine. "This is terrific!" you say. Then one day you go to work and the foreman says, "Here's your termination notice."

Now it's, "Lord! What are You doing to me? This is terrible!" But maybe God has a better job for you, and you weren't looking for it. Now you are! God couldn't bring you to the better position until He upset the old conditions. Now you're open and listening to what God has to say. The Father delights in giving good things to His children, just as a parent loves to give some wonderful gift to his child.

We have one son who's always been difficult to please. Buy him a new shirt and he'll say, "Does it match my slacks?" Buy him new shoes and he'll say, "Why did you get that style?" Sometimes God has a hard time giving us gifts, too. What a disappointment when you give a truly wonderful gift to someone you love, and he or she barely acknowledges it. That isn't a response anyone appreciates, especially God.

But became vain in their imaginations, and their foolish heart was darkened. Professing themselves to be wise, they became fools (1:21b-22). Our imaginations often focus on the empty things of the world, and much of our mental power is exercised on vain fantasies. How much better when our hearts and minds are filled with God, His Word, and His love. The wisdom of the world is foolishness to God. Many times we profess

ourselves to be wise and actually become fools by the
theories that we believe and follow.

**And changed the glory of the incorruptible God
into an image made like to corruptible man** (1:23a).
The men of the world tried to make an image of God by
fashioning it in the form of man.

**And to birds, and four-footed beasts, and creep-
ing things** (1:23b). Have you ever seen the grotesque
images of past civilizations or the awful images in India
today that are worshiped as God? Quite often the statues
are part man and part animal. How tragic and foolish!
Yet people worship these things and say, "That's God."

Now we come to the first mention of being "given
up" by God. **Wherefore God also gave them up to
uncleanness [sexual uncleanness or impurity]
through the lusts of their own hearts, to dishonor
their own bodies between themselves** (1:24). Whenever man fashions an image of God in the form of a
man, he brings God even below his own level. When a
man puts eyes and ears on an idol, it still can't see or
hear. Setting God below his own level creates moral
depravity in man, for he loses his high ideals and becomes like his god. His god is *less* than man, thus his
god becomes in his mind a base creature.

The ritual worship of false gods was often done through
fertility rites and practices. In Paul's time, the great
temple of Aphrodite stood on the Acropolis in Corinth.
The priestesses of this temple were prostitutes who came
into the city nightly. The Corinthians "worshiped"
Aphrodite through sexual rites, and the profit supported
their religion. Man degrades himself whenever he
worships anything other than the true and living God.
So, man is given up by God and given over to
"uncleanness."

Who changed the truth of God into a lie (1:25a). Man has to live with himself, so he rationalizes his evil deeds in order to ease his conscience. But to do that he has to change his perception of God. He challenges God's Word and claims, "The Bible isn't really the inspired Word of God." Or he underestimates Him saying, "God doesn't care. He isn't really concerned."

In Paul's day some men believed that the body was completely separate from God's concern. These men taught that you must worship God in the realm of the spirit, but you could do whatever you pleased with your body. Such a teaching changes the truth of God into a lie, to accommodate the lusts of the flesh.

And worshipped and served the creature more than the Creator (1:25b). Men are doing the same thing today as in Paul's day. They're worshiping and serving the works of their own hands rather than the Creator of all things. Idolatry, one of the most common of all sins, is the obsession for the things made by men's hands. The idolator cannot rest until he possesses the object of his desire. **For this cause God gave them up** (1:26a).

Paul also tells us that **God gave them up unto vile affections: for even their women did change the natural use into that which is against nature: and likewise also the men, leaving the natural use of the woman, burned in their lust one toward another** (1:26-27). Lesbianism and homosexuality follow whenever God gives up women and men to the things they desire. Don't tell me that God created a homosexual that way. That's changing the truth of God into a lie. Man becomes perverted because he doesn't want to retain God in his mind. He refuses to glorify God as God, and he seeks to make a god after himself. God gives him up to these vile affections, because he has rejected the truth of God within his own heart.

But if a person will return and submit himself to the truth, Jesus will free him from that power and manner of life. He came to set the captive free!

Even as they did not like to retain God in their knowledge, God gave them over to a reprobate mind, to do those things which are not convenient [ought not to be done]; being filled with all unrighteousness, fornication, wickedness, covetousness, maliciousness; full of envy, murder, debate, deceit, malignity; whisperers, backbiters, haters of God, despiteful, proud, boasters, inventors of evil things, disobedient to parents, without understanding, covenant breakers, without natural affection, implacable, unmerciful (1:28-31).

This passage shows the sad picture of society today. People have sought to rule God out of their consciences. So, God has given them up to these vile practices. These sins will manifest themselves whenever a society turns its back upon God and seeks independence from Him. Whoever rejects Jesus Christ will find himself going downhill fast, doing things he never dreamed of, and losing any scruples against doing them.

Who knowing the judgment of God, that they which commit such things are worthy of death, not only do the same, but have pleasure in them that do them (1:32). Many people hold a prideful view of themselves, as the Pharisee who said, "God, I thank thee, that I am not as other men" (Luke 18:11). They feel smug because they're innocent of some of the grosser forms of sin. Yet, they go to a movie or watch a TV program as actors portray these vile things, and they actually enjoy or "have pleasure in them that do them." We need to take great care not to sow to our flesh in any way. "For he that soweth to his flesh shall of the flesh reap corruption" (Galatians 6:8).

CHAPTER 2
GOD'S JUSTICE

There is no break in Paul's writing between Chapters 1 and 2, and he continues in the next verse, **Therefore thou art inexcusable, O man, whosoever thou art that judgest: for wherein thou judgest another, thou condemnest thyself; for thou that judgest doest the same things** (2:1). We may judge someone else's sins, but so often we're guilty of the very same act.

Watching television and movies can be dangerous. Often a person receives vicarious pleasure from watching the violence and corruption on the screen. He wouldn't think of doing such things himself, but when he sees them portrayed on a screen he drinks it all in. He's as guilty as the people he's watching, because he's mentally indulging in the same practices.

But we are sure that the judgment of God is according to truth against them which commit such things (2:2). God's judgment will be according to truth, because He'll judge not only men's actions but the motives that prompted the actions.

Many times after committing a crime, a man will make up an excuse to justify what he's done. As he gives you his explanation, he sounds like he really is innocent. However, he made up the story after the fact to justify himself and avoid punishment.

God told Ezekiel, "Dig a hole through the wall, go in, and take a look around the house of Israel." Ezekiel went in and saw many filthy pictures, detestable animals, and idols upon the walls. The Lord said, "You're seeing the insides of the minds of men" (Ezekiel 8:8-12).

Some day you may stand before God in heaven saying, "I didn't intend to cause any harm." He could say, "Let's review the thoughts that were in your mind at that moment." The Bible says, "All things are naked and opened unto the eyes of him with whom we have to do" (Hebrews 4:13b). You can't hide from God. He knows the secret motives of your heart, and His judgment will be according to the absolute truth.

Or despisest thou the riches of his goodness and forbearance and longsuffering; not knowing that the goodness of God leadeth thee to repentance? (2:4). Men so often mistake the patience of God as a weakness or, worse yet, as approval. A man says, "If there is a God in heaven, let Him strike me dead!" He shakes his fist at God. When he isn't struck dead, he says, "I told you. There is no God." How foolish! A person may be lulled into believing that God doesn't care or that He even approves of his sins, because God's judgment isn't immediate. By misinterpreting the patience of God as "getting by with it," a man shows despite toward the goodness of God and fools himself.

The goodness of God leads a man to repentance. So many times a preacher tries to get a sinner to repent by shaking him over hell and emphasizing the wrath of God. In reality, knowing how much he deserves the judgment and wrath of God, yet realizing the goodness, forbearance, and longsuffering of God, leads a man to repent.

The day of judgment will come and all secrets will be revealed. **But after thy hardness and impenitent heart treasurest up unto thyself wrath against the day of wrath and revelation of the righteous judgment of God** (2:5). That's why I pray, "Remember not the sins of my youth" (Psalm 25:7a). That's why David prayed, "Have mercy upon me, O God... according unto the multitude of thy tender mercies blot out my transgressions" (Psalm 51:1). As a sinner David didn't say, "Have *justice* on me, O God."

God will render to every man according to his deeds (2:6). By continuing to sin, a person is storing up a huge reservoir of judgment that will finally burst and carry him off in the torrent. **To them who by patient continuance in well doing seek for glory and honour and immortality, God will reward with eternal life. But unto them that are contentious, and do not obey the truth, but obey unrighteousness, indignation and wrath, tribulation and anguish, upon every soul of man that doeth evil, of the Jew first, and also of the Gentile; but glory, honour, and peace, to every man that worketh good, to the Jew first, and also to the Gentile** (2:7-10).

For there is no respect of persons with God (2:11). In this particular dispensation God deals equally with all men, Jews and Gentiles. If you're following Christ, He'll bless and reward you. If you harden your heart against Him by following your own path, then God will judge you regardless of whether you're a Jew or a Gentile. Your nationality won't make the day of judgment any easier for you, because God doesn't show any favoritism.

For as many as have sinned without law shall also perish without law: and as many as have sinned in the law shall be judged by the law (2:12). Those who have never heard about Jesus Christ will be judged according to the knowledge that they have had. If they didn't have the Law of Moses, they'll be judged apart from the Law.

(For not the hearers of the law are just before God, but the doers of the law shall be justified. For when the Gentiles, which have not the law, do by nature the things contained in the law, these, having not the law, are a law unto themselves: which show the work of the law written in their hearts, their conscience also

bearing witness, and their thoughts the meanwhile accusing or else excusing one another) (2:13-15).

God has given each person a basic sense of right and wrong. This standard is written upon the tablet of his heart, and his thoughts are either accusing or excusing him. What will God judge? **The secrets of men by Jesus Christ according to my gospel** (2:16).

Behold, thou art called a Jew, and restest in the law, and makest thy boast of God, and knowest his will, and approvest the things that are more excellent, being instructed out of the law; and art confident that thou thyself art a guide of the blind, a light of them which are in darkness, an instructor of the foolish, a teacher of babes, which hast the form of knowledge and of the truth in the law. Thou therefore which teachest another, teachest thou not thyself? Thou that preachest a man should not steal, dost thou steal? Thou that sayest a man should not commit adultery, dost thou commit adultery? Thou that abhorrest idols, dost thou commit sacrilege? Thou that makest thy boast of the law, through breaking the law dishonourest thou God? (2:17-23).

Paul was addressing himself to the Jews who had the Law of Moses and were boasting in it. "We have the Law and know the things that are right. We're a light to those in darkness and a guide to the blind." The Jews stood as the moral and spiritual teachers of the world.

But Paul said, "Wait a minute! You teach that a man shouldn't steal, but do you covet your neighbor's goods? You teach that a man shouldn't commit adultery, but do you think about it yourself? You teach that a man shouldn't worship idols, but do you secretly worship idols in your heart?"

Paul was pointing out that the true intent of the Law is to govern and judge the attitudes of men more than their actions. This is the very thing that Jesus pointed out in the

Sermon on the Mount (Matthew 5:17-18). Using five examples, He showed how the Law was being misinterpreted by the scribes and Pharisees and what God meant when He gave it. In each case, the scribes were applying the Law to a man's *actions* when God was judging his *attitudes*. The whole purpose of the Law was voided by their misinterpretation.

By applying the Law only to actions, the scribes felt very self-righteous. However, the Law's purpose was to make the whole world guilty before God by revealing sin and, thus, drive men to the grace of God in Jesus Christ. By misunderstanding the intent of the Law, the reaction of the scribes in their smugness and self-righteousness was exactly the opposite of what God intended.

As a result, **the name of God is blasphemed among the Gentiles through you, as it is written. For circumcision verily profiteth, if thou keep the law: but if thou be a breaker of the law, thy circumcision is made uncircumcision** (2:24-25). The Jews were trusting in the Mosaic ritual of circumcision for their salvation, but their disobedience of the spirit of the Law invalidated the ritual.

It's wrong to trust in a ritual; rituals such as baptism, for salvation. Unfortunately, the so-called salvation of many people is based on the water sprinkled on their heads as infants. These people don't even remember the event, but they have a certificate that proves it happened. Such a religious ritual is meaningless in terms of salvation. Our relationship with God is totally dependent upon a *living, active* faith in Jesus Christ.

You may say, "When I was baptized, they put me all the way under. None of that sprinkling for me!" If you're not walking according to God's will, the ritual means nothing, even if you were baptized in the deepest ocean. Your heart determines your salvation, and your present life can invalidate the meaning of any ritual you may have experienced.

Paul says that the benefit of circumcision is removed by disobedience to the Law of God. **For circumcision verily profiteth, if thou keep the law: but if thou be a breaker of the law, thy circumcision is made uncircumcision. Therefore if the uncircumcision keep the righteousness of the law, shall not his uncircumcision be counted for circumcision?** (2:25-26). The crucial issue isn't ritual but obedience to God.

Personally, I don't agree with any denomination claiming that a person cannot be saved until he is baptized. Does baptism save? No. The work of God in a man's heart is what counts. Salvation rests upon the work of Jesus Christ on the Cross.

And shall not uncircumcision which is by nature, if it fulfil the law, judge thee, who by the letter and circumcision dost transgress the law? For he is not a Jew which is one outwardly; neither is that circumcision, which is outward in the flesh: but he is a Jew, which is one inwardly; and circumcision is that of the heart, in the spirit, and not in the letter; whose praise is not of men, but of God (2:27-29).

Circumcision was intended to signify a people who would deny their flesh and live after the Spirit. The significance of the rite could be totally negated by a man if he continued to live after the flesh. Likewise, baptism symbolizes the death of the old nature and the new life of the Spirit. The proof of this work of God is in a person's life, not in any ritual.

What advantage then hath the Jew? or what profit is there of circumcision? (3:1). If circumcision can't get me points in heaven, then what advantage do I have as a Jew? Paul said, **Much every way: chiefly, because that unto them were committed the oracles of God** (3:2). God committed His Word to the Jews in their native language. Those who read Hebrew could read God's Word.

We owe a great deal to the Jews for preserving the Word of God with such diligence and accuracy. Prior to the discovery of the Dead Sea Scrolls in 1947, the oldest complete Hebrew manuscript of the Old Testament was dated about A.D. 900. The Dead Sea Isaiah Scroll is dated about 200 B.C. When the Isaiah Scroll was translated, it was found to have no major changes from the text we already possessed. The Jewish scribes had faithfully and accurately copied the Word of God throughout the Old Testament period.

What if some [of them] did not believe? shall their unbelief make the faith of God without effect? (3:3). This is an interesting speculation. A man may claim to be an unbeliever. That doesn't change the truth. Suppose that he went into a math class. The teacher had written on the board, "2 + 2 = 4". He says, "Wait a minute! I don't believe that two plus two equals four." His opinion won't change the fact. Whether he believes or not doesn't alter the truth.

The truth will stand, and it isn't without effect because a person doesn't believe it. Similarly, a man cannot add to God by accepting the truth. When a sinner repents and accepts Christ, God doesn't say, "Oh, good! Another one on our side." He doesn't need us. He can live very well without us. He loves us, and because He loves us He draws us unto Himself. We're the ones who gain and are blessed. It's so wonderful that God pursues this relationship with us when He has nothing to gain by it.

For what if some did not believe? Shall their unbelief make the faith of God without effect? God forbid: yea, let God be true, but every man a liar; as it is written, That thou mightest be justified in thy sayings, and mightest overcome when thou art judged. But if our unrighteousness commend the righteousness of God, what shall we say? Is God unrighteous who taketh vengeance? (I speak as a man) (3:3-5).

A person may claim, "God said that we're all sinners in Romans 3:23. By being a sinner I'm only proving that God told the truth. Why should God take vengeance on me because I'm proving His truth?" Oh, the stupid reasoning of man! How often we find ourselves addressing these nonsensical arguments. Paul said, **God forbid [perish the thought]: for then how shall God judge the world? For if the truth of God hath more abounded through my lie unto his glory; why yet am I also judged as a sinner?** (3:6-7).

Some preachers tell stories packed with emotion in an attempt to turn people to Christ. There's no truth to the story, but it's persuasive and turns people from their sins. "Some might say, "Why would God judge a preacher for lying? Look at the good that has come from it." But the end doesn't justify the means. Jesus said, "Many will say to me in that day, Lord, Lord, have we not prophesied in thy name? and in thy name have cast out devils? and in thy name done many wonderful works? And then will I profess unto them, I never knew you: depart from me, ye that work iniquity" (Matthew 7:22-23).

Some Christians were slanderously reported to have said, "Let us do evil that good may come." Paul characterized such people as those **whose damnation is just** (3:8). The evil of man and the righteousness of God stand in brilliant contrast. Take the case of Tex Watson, a convicted murderer and former member of the Charles Manson family. Tex Watson is now a brother in Christ. How his conversion magnifies the grace of God. But should we do wicked things so we can magnify the grace of God? Never! One of the most glorious of all testimonies is obeying God's will. That kind of testimony thrills God's heart.

What then? are we better than they? No, in no wise: for we have before proved both Jews and Gentiles, that they are all under sin; as it is written, There is none righteous, no, not one (3:9-10).

Paul goes on to describe these deceivers who encouraged evil so that more of God's grace would be given.

There is none that understandeth, there is none that seeketh after God. They are all gone out of the way, they are together become unprofitable; there is none that doeth good, no, not one. Their throat is an open sepulchre; with their tongues they have used deceit; the poison of asps is under their lips: whose mouth is full of cursing and bitterness: their feet are swift to shed blood: destruction and misery are in their ways: and the way of peace have they not known: there is no fear of God before their eyes. Now we know that what things soever the law saith, it saith to them who are under the law:

**that every mouth may be stopped, and all the world
may become guilty before God. Therefore by the
deeds of the law there shall no flesh be justified in
his sight: for by the law is the knowledge of sin**
(3:11-20).

No one can be justified by the Law of Moses, the Ten
Commandments. We're already guilty before we even
start. The Law wasn't given to justify us, but to expose
our innate sinfulness. It reveals the fact that the whole
world is guilty before God.

The Jews had misinterpreted the Law to such an ex-
tent that they felt self-righteous. The religious leaders
were teaching that a man could actually keep the Law,
because their idea of obedience was by outward obser-
vance only. But in the Sermon on the Mount Jesus pointed
out that the Law was spiritual and that all men had
already violated it. Jesus showed that the Law governs
the inner attitudes of men as well as their outward actions. Though the Jews' actions may have been blameless, their attitudes were evil. For example, though they
hadn't committed adultery, they had lusted in their hearts.
So, they were guilty of violating the Law.

The Law condemns all of us, and it points all of us to
the only hope of salvation that we have—the grace and
mercy of God and the forgiveness of our sins through
Jesus Christ.

**But now the righteousness of God without the
law is manifested, being witnessed by the law and
the prophets; even the righteousness of God which
is by faith of Jesus Christ unto all and upon all
them that believe: for there is no difference** (3:21-
22). No difference exists between Jew and Gentile in
terms of salvation. Each one who believes in Jesus Christ
is justified from all the sins he has ever committed.

"Justified" is a beautiful word meaning *just as if I'd never done it.* When I stand before Him cleansed by the blood of Jesus Christ, God looks at me as though the disobedience and sins of the past had never happened. God credits my faith in Him as righteousness. My hope is in the sustaining power and grace of God through His Holy Spirit. Jesus said, "I am the vine, ye are the branches: He that abideth in me, and I in him, the same bringeth forth much fruit: for without me ye can do nothing" (John 15:5). Apart from Christ I have no justification before God.

When I abide in Christ, my salvation and relationship with God doesn't vary. Years ago my relationship with Him was unstable in my own mind, because I tried to make it depend upon my good works. As a child I was taught that I shouldn't go to movies, dance, smoke cigarettes, or drink liquor. So I have abstained from all those things, but as a child I couldn't understand why God was blessing some kids at church more than He was blessing me. They were sneaking off to the Saturday matinee and smoking cigarettes. "God, I'm so good and they're such sneaks!" I was approaching God on the basis of my good works, but I wasn't so good in my thoughts. When the other kids were heading to the matinee, I really wanted to see Pinocchio or Snow White with them. How I wished I hadn't been brought up in that strict church. I longed for those things in my heart, but I wouldn't do them.

My Sunday school teachers told me the story of a little boy who went to the movies and said, "Jesus, please wait outside. I'll be back in about an hour and a half." I was told never to go anywhere I couldn't take the Lord. "If the Lord should come while you're at the movies, He'll leave you behind. When you come out, you may find the Church is raptured and you've been left." The first movie I finally went to see was agony. The whole time I thought, "What if the Lord comes while I'm sitting here? What if the rapture takes place?" I wanted to get up and leave!

Eventually, God in His grace caused me to realize that true righteousness isn't based on rules but on my faith in Jesus Christ. My relationship with God then stabilized. I certainly don't do the right thing in every situation. For example, I don't always tolerate abuse and won't always turn the other cheek. Thank God that my faults don't alter my faith in Jesus. I still believe in Him and love Him with all my heart. When I do wrong He speaks to me about it, and He teaches me to lean a little harder on Him instead of on myself.

God has brought me into a new righteousness based upon His faithfulness to keep His Word. There's never a problem on that basis, because I know that God is faithful and will always keep His word.

For all have sinned, and come short of the glory of God (3:23). Some may come closer than others, but all have come short of God's standard. As an illustration, suppose that we're sailing to Hawaii and the boat capsizes midway. We start swimming for shore. Some are very weak swimmers and sink within the first hundred yards. Some don't go down until the first mile. Some are strong enough to swim five miles before they go down, but all come short of reaching land.

Being justified freely by his grace through the redemption that is in Christ Jesus (3:24). We can only be justified before God by His grace in the redemption purchased for us by Jesus Christ.

Whom God has set forth to be a propitiation through faith in his blood, to declare his righteousness for the remission of sins that are past, through the forbearance of God; to declare, I say, at this time his righteousness: that he might be

just, and the justifier of him which believeth in Jesus (3:25-26).

In order to forgive you, God must have a just basis of forgiveness. That basis of forgiveness is the substitution of Christ for you, the sinner. Jesus took your sins and bore your guilt. God had declared, "The soul that sinneth, it shall die" (Ezekiel 18:20). Jesus died in your place and bore the judgment of your guilt. Thus, He can offer the forgiveness of your sins and the cleansing of your past. He can justify you before God of any wrong you have ever done. That's God's good news. Paul said, "For I am not ashamed of the gospel of Christ: for it is the power of God unto salvation" (Romans 1:16a).

Where is boasting then? It is excluded. By what law? of works? Nay: but by the law of faith. Therefore, we conclude that a man is justified by faith without the deeds of the law (3:27-28). Salvation is by faith and it completely eliminates any boasting by us.

> And when, before the throne, I stand in Him complete,
> "Jesus died my soul to save," my lips shall still repeat.
> Jesus paid it all, all to Him I owe;
> Sin had left a crimson stain,
> He washed it white as snow.[1]

What a glorious day it will be when Jesus presents me "faultless before the presence of his glory with exceeding joy" (Jude 24b). I won't be able to say, "I was such a faithful and strong Christian! I really held on to the end!" No! Boasting is eliminated, because my salvation has become God's work.

The Bible says, "Ye are complete in him" (Colossians 2:10a). "Complete" means "perfect." You can't improve on

---

[1] From *Jesus Paid It All* by Mrs. H.M. Hall.

perfection. Having begun in the Spirit, you must continue to walk in faith. God sees you in that state of perfection as you abide in Christ.

Is he the God of the Jews only? Is he not also of the Gentiles? Yes, of the Gentiles also: seeing it is one God, who shall justify the circumcision by faith, and uncircumcision through faith (3:29-30). The Jews thought that they possessed God exclusively. Not so. All men may approach God now. The rituals of the past no longer matter, for faith in Christ is the key to justification.

However, faith doesn't cancel the Law of Moses. It actually supports the purpose of the Law. **Do we then make void the law through faith? God forbid: yea, we establish the law** (3:31). The Law was given to show that all the world stands guilty before God. Salvation by faith eliminates all human boasting and shows us that we cannot save ourselves by works. Faith brings us to the same realization as the Law, and so it establishes the Law.

CHAPTER 4
ABRAHAM AND FAITH

In Chapter 4 of Romans Paul talks about the righteousness that God has established through faith. This righteousness isn't accomplished by outward obedience to the Law of Moses, but upon the principle of faith. Righteousness through faith eliminates any boasting on man's behalf. "Where is boasting then? It is excluded. By what law? of works? Nay: but by the law of faith" (Romans 3:27).

My salvation is a work of God. I can't boast in my own works, because my salvation is God's work in me. He did it and I believed it. God counts my faith in the righteousness of Christ as my own righteousness.

In Chapter 4 Paul also emphasizes that justification by faith isn't a new concept with God. He explains that God had established the principle of faith with Abraham, the father of the Jewish nation, long before the Mosaic Law was ever given.

What shall we say then that Abraham our father, as pertaining to the flesh, hath found? (4:1). What did Abraham, the physical father of the Jews, discover about faith and justification?

For if Abraham were justified by works, he hath whereof to glory; but not before God. For what saith the scripture? Abraham believed God, and it was counted unto him for righteousness (4:2-3). If Abraham was justified by obediently leaving his home by Babylon to look for the Promised Land or by offering his son Isaac as a sacrifice, then he would have been able to boast in himself. He could have said, "I left my home and was willing to give up everything, even my son, to follow God. I'm really righteous!" However, Abraham was justified solely by faith, not by works.

This same principle of justification by faith is true in our own salvation. If we were justified by our works, we could glory in ourselves and, thus, our boasting wouldn't be in God's work. For this reason Paul said, "God forbid that I should glory, save in the cross of our Lord Jesus Christ" (Galatians 6:14a). Our only place of boasting is in the Cross. Jesus said, "So you also, when you have done everything you were commanded to do, should say, We are unworthy servants, for we have done only what was our duty" (Luke 17:10).

Glory for my salvation should always be given to God, yet my flesh delights in self-glory. How I'd love to take credit for my salvation, and I keep trying! Every time I say, "God, there must be some good in me somewhere!" He lets me fall flat on my face. There's nothing in my flesh about which I can glory.

Paul repeats this same truth in Chapter 7. "I know that in me (that is, in my flesh) dwelleth no good thing" (Romans 7:18a). If you haven't discovered this fact yet, you will. God doesn't plan to redeem your flesh; He condemns your flesh to the Cross. He must change you from this corruptible body into an incorruptible one before you can enter into the eternal kingdom. "This corruptible [perishable] must put on incorruption [imperishable], and this mortal must put on immortality" (I Corinthians 15:53).

Even when I know that no good dwells in my flesh, I often say, "Lord, surely I can conquer this problem. Give me a chance and I'll do better. I promise that I won't fail again." Every promise of doing better and being more faithful is doomed to failure, because it's rooted in the confidence of my flesh. My boasting and confidence must be in Jesus Christ and His finished work for me.

The concept of righteousness by faith is quite foreign to us. We often attempt to achieve righteousness by the *do's and don'ts* of Christian behavior, and we're soon legislating our own religious laws. Since there are always amendments and modifications, the list eventually becomes so long that no one can keep up with it.

If I have followed the rule of keeping my temper and have blessed others when I was abused, I feel very confident and begin to boast of conquering another area of my old nature. I feel very good, until I lose my cool and yell at my kids. Then I cry, "O God! I'm a miserable failure! I promised that I'd never do that again." I now feel so miserable and alienated from God.

Why did God establish the principle of righteousness by faith? It's the only way that my relationship with Him can remain constant in spite of my human failures.

The Mosaic Law failed to bring righteousness because its benefits depended upon man's obedience. "The man who obeys them will live by them" (Leviticus 18:5). The Law's fulfillment was based on man's flesh, but his flesh is weak. The Law didn't fail. Man failed. So God has established a new basis for righteousness: faith in Jesus Christ. Jesus has promised to cleanse a man from all sin and to present him faultless before the Father.

This New Covenant is based on God's faithfulness to keep His word. I fulfill my part of the bargain by trusting in God through faith in Jesus Christ. My righteous standing is complete once I stop trying to justify myself before God and rest where God is resting—in the finished work of Jesus Christ. (The Bible explains more about this "rest" in Hebrews 4.)

Now to him that worketh is the reward not reckoned of grace, but of debt (4:4). If righteousness was credited to a man for his works, then God would owe him the reward of salvation. The Jehovah's Witnesses believe that they can work for their righteousness by door-to-door witnessing. Trusting in a righteousness that goes back to the Law, they seek to put God in debt to them. However, God will never be any man's debtor.

When I work for an employer, he is legally obligated to pay me my wages. But a right relationship with God is a gift that I do not, cannot, and never will deserve. This gift demonstrates the grace of God, as He gives me what I could never earn: perfect righteousness.

But to him that worketh not, but believeth on him that justifieth the ungodly, his faith is counted for righteousness (4:5). Some people may look at this statement as almost heretical, but it's scriptural. They may protest that justification by faith is a dangerous thing to preach. "Christians will become lazy. They'll sit around believing in the Lord and do nothing." However, it's impossible to believe in Jesus Christ and do nothing. True faith will spark a tremendous response in a man.

The works of a Christian are in no way intended to make him holier or more righteous before God. One of the curses in the Church throughout the centuries has been the holier-than-thou attitude. They come to you with dreamy eyes and say, "Brother, are you ready for the secrets of God that have been made known to me?" That super-spiritual attitude is a curse among Christians.

My works don't add a whit to my righteousness. God has imputed to me the righteousness of Jesus Christ, and trying to improve on it is sheer folly. The fullness of the Godhead bodily dwells in Christ, and I'm complete in Him. (Colossians 2:9-10)

Then what are my works as a believer? Just the glorious and natural response of my heart to the goodness, grace, and love of God. Paul said, "The love of Christ constraineth [compels] me" (II Corinthians 5:14). Love drives me to do whatever I can for Him.

Love is the highest motivating force, and it's the only acceptable motive for any true service for God. If love doesn't motivate me in my service for God, I might as well stop. If I think that my Christian service is making me holier or more righteous than others, I'm badly mistaken. "And though I bestow all my goods to feed the poor, and though I give my body to be burned, and have not love, it profiteth me nothing" (I Corinthians 13:3).

Many times the urgings from the pulpit prompt people to serve the Lord for rewards. I was guilty of doing that for years. "I'll give you a giant lollipop if you bring ten kids to Sunday school." However, the entire work-reward concept is carnal, not spiritual. By appealing to this carnal motive, many pastors have created a spirit of competitiveness within their congregations. Though a person may work himself to death, he'll receive nothing for his carnal efforts, except perhaps some personal glory and applause when he collects his giant lollipop.

Not striving to do God's work doesn't mean that I'm spiritually lazy. It usually means that I'm doing more than ever, but my motivation is God's great love. Rewards could never have prompted me to do the things I've done. As Paul said, "Neither count I my life dear unto myself" (Acts 20:24a). To please and serve Christ becomes the joy, desire, and delight of my life, because He loves me so much.

Even as David also describeth the blessedness of the man, unto whom God imputeth righteousness without works, saying, Blessed are they whose iniquities are forgiven, and whose sins are covered. Blessed is the man to whom the Lord will not impute sin (4:6-8). The word "blessed" means "Oh, how happy!" How happy is the man to whom the Lord will not impute iniquity.

Did you know that God no longer charges sin against you if you're believing in Jesus Christ? "If we walk in the light, as he is in the light, we have fellowship one with another, and the blood of Jesus Christ his Son continually cleanses us from all sin... If any man sin, we have an advocate with the Father, Jesus Christ the righteous: and he is the propitiation for our sins" (I John 1:7, 2:1b-2a).

Cometh this blessedness then upon the circumcision only? (4:9a). Is this blessedness of divine forgiveness just for the Jew? **Or in uncircumcision? Not in circumcision, but in uncircumcision** (4:10b). To the Jews circumcision was the most important ritual that a man could experience. According to their teaching, God wouldn't accept an uncircumcised man. Yet Paul says that faith, not circumcision, gave Abraham his standing before God. God credited his faith for righteousness while Abraham was still uncircumcised.

And he received the sign of circumcision, a seal of the righteousness of the faith which he had yet being uncircumcised: that he might be the father of all them that believe, though they be not circumcised; that righteousness might be imputed unto them [Gentiles] also: and the father of circumcision to them who are not of the circumcision only, but who also walk in the steps of that faith of our father Abraham, which he had being yet uncircumcised (4:11-12).

God has imparted perfect righteousness to me, a sinner, totally apart from works and rituals. The bread and wine of the Lord's Supper are only a memorial. They will not save me. The water of baptism is only a symbol. It will not save me. Salvation is the work of God within my heart through faith in Jesus Christ alone.

For the promise, that he should be the heir of the world, was not to Abraham, or to his seed, through the law (4:13a). Abraham lived 400 years before the Mosaic Law was given. His righteousness must have been apart from the Law, since the Law didn't even exist yet.

But through the righteousness of faith. For if they which are of the law be heirs, faith is made void, and the promise made of none effect: because the law worketh wrath: for where no law is, there is no trans-

gression (4:13b-15). A man can't transgress a law that doesn't exist. So, mankind couldn't violate the Law until it had been given.

Therefore it [our righteousness] is of faith, that it might be by grace; to the end the promise might be sure (4:16a). A righteousness predicated upon your works could never be sure. Neither could it be sure if it depended upon your faithfulness. Because God wants you to be assured of your salvation, He promises to save you if you'll just believe in His Son Jesus Christ and His finished work for you on the cross. Salvation isn't premised on your works but on His work, not on your faithfulness but on His faithfulness. Only thus can your salvation be sure.

The guarantee of your salvation is certain. You don't need to constantly worry yourself with doubts and questions, such as, "Did I confess everything today? Forgive everybody? Love everybody? If I go to sleep and die tonight, will I find myself in hell?" Not knowing for certain whether you're saved would be miserable. Your attitude would be, "I hope I've done my best. I hope I haven't sinned. I hope..." You'd never have any confidence in your salvation, whereas God wants you to have confidence and certainty. So, He has established His New Covenant on the basis of faith in the complete work of Christ. Your salvation is secure and you don't have to worry, because Jesus has covered your sins of the past, present, and future.

To the end the promise might be sure to all the seed; not to that only which is of the law, but to that also which is of the faith of Abraham; who is the father of us all (4:16). Abraham is my father not in the ancestral but in the spiritual sense. He's the father of all who believe in God and are accounted righteous by their faith in Christ.

(As it is written, I have made thee a father of many nations,) before him whom he believed, even God, who quickeneth the dead, and calleth those things which be not as though they were (4:17).

Long before Abraham had fathered Isaac, God spoke to him as though his son already existed. I'm greatly comforted when God speaks about me as righteous, justified, glorified, holy, pure, and sanctified completely. God can talk about such things before they exist, because He knows they will exist. Jesus Christ will present me before the Father "faultless... with exceeding joy" (Jude 24). In the Bible God talks about my future state as a certainty. My dwelling with Him eternally is a fact to Him, just as Abraham's unborn son was a fact. Abraham **against hope believed in hope, that he might become the father of many nations, according to that which was spoken, So shall thy seed be** (4:18).

We now come to the four keys of Abraham's faith. **And being not weak in faith, he considered not his own body now dead, when he was about an hundred years old, neither yet the deadness of Sarah's womb** (4:19). Ignoring the physical limitations of the situation was the first key of Abraham's faith.

Whenever I'm faced with a problem, I usually try to work out my own solution. As long as I can devise a plan, I feel confident. However, when a situation seems to have no solution, I start to worry. If I can't figure it out, how will God be able to solve it?

So often when I've worked out a possible solution in my mind, I then begin to direct God in my prayers according to my planned solution. At this point my prayers become direction prayers rather than direct prayers. God does answer prayer, but He often refuses to follow my directions.

Too often we trust in human evaluations and the analysis from the laboratory. Is the tumor malignant? The report says that it's benign, so we praise the Lord. But should word of malignancy come, we panic and give up all hope. We're only seeing the human possibilities.

Sarah could have called on the doctor and said, "My husband and I want a son of our own. However, I went through menopause about 30 years ago."

The doctor would have said, "Sarah, you're dreaming!"

Can you imagine Abraham coming in for his annual checkup saying, "Sarah and I want a son. Can you give me some vitamins or something?"

"No chance," the doctor says. "You're almost 100 years old and your wife is past 90. A son now? Abraham, forget it. That's humanly impossible!" God's promise to Abraham was humanly impossible to fulfill, but Abraham simply ignored the natural considerations.

When God is the working agent, any talk of limitations or difficulty is absurd. For example, consider the events in II Kings 7:1-20. When the Syrians besieged the city of Samaria and cut off all their supplies, the conditions became hopeless. The people, starving to death, resorted to eating their own children. A donkey's head sold for 80 shekels on about two pounds of silver.

When the king and his officer visited the home of Elisha, the prophet promised a complete reversal of circumstances. He said, "Tomorrow, about this time, a seah [seven quarts] of flour will sell for a shekel [65 cents] and two seahs of barley for a shekel at the gate of Samaria."

The king's officer said, "Elisha, even if the Lord would make windows in heaven, could such a thing ever be?" The prophet replied, "Behold, you will see it with your own eyes, but you will not eat it." Such a provision sounded so impossible under the circumstances that the officer didn't believe it.

Such is the price of unbelief. It robs you of the blessings God has already provided. So often we look for the ways that God might work—"If God would open windows in heaven" — but we don't need to understand the ways of the Lord. All we need is to believe and trust in Him.

The second key to Abraham's faith was not staggering in unbelief at the promises of God. **He staggered not at the promise of God through unbelief** (4:20a). How many times we stagger at God's promises through unbelief! God's promises often seem too good to be true. I can accept what God did for Elijah and Paul, but I can't believe that He would do it for me.

The Bible says, "He has given us exceeding great and precious promises" (II Peter 1:4a). One of these promises is "My God will meet all your needs according to his riches in glory by Christ Jesus" (Philippians 4:19). The promises of God are so great that our belief in them is prone to waver, and we hesitate rather than confidently claim them.

Abraham didn't waver, **but was strong in faith, giving glory to God** (4:20b). This was the third key to Abraham's faith. He was praising and thanking God for a son even before Sarah was pregnant.

Years ago while pastoring in another area, I was working at a supermarket to meet the family's needs. We had three children and the church only paid twenty dollars a week.

My mother-in-law had died in Phoenix, and we went there to take care of the funeral arrangements. While I was gone my union dues at the supermarket lapsed. When I returned to pay them, the union had attached a fifty dollar fine. I couldn't afford to pay the fine plus the dues. I was in a bind, because the union wouldn't let me work, and I couldn't get the money without the work.

Since my income from the supermarket had stopped, things were pretty tough and I became discouraged. I've always believed in keeping my accounts up to date as a witness for Jesus Christ. Now for the first time in my life I started receiving letters from my creditors.

One morning I got up and totaled our debts. They came to $416.00. I laid them before the Lord, but I was very disheartened. "Where in the world am I ever going to get $416.00?"

About that time the phone rang. I picked it up, and a friend said, "Chuck, I'm calling to let you know that I put a check in the mail for you. I sent it special delivery, and you should get it tomorrow morning. It's for $425.00."

Was I ever elated! I ran into the kitchen, grabbed my wife, and danced her around the room. I was praising the Lord. "Victory! Bless God! Hallelujah! We'll be out of debt! We even have enough money to go out for dinner!"

Later, after I had settled down again, God began speaking to me. "How do you know that he sent the money to you?"

"Lord, I've known my friend for many years. He wouldn't call me unless he'd done it. I trust his word, Lord."

"Very interesting," said the Lord. "You had My word this morning that I would provide the money, but I didn't see you dancing your wife around the kitchen. Instead, you were down in the mouth and blue. Now that you have a man's word for the money, you're all excited. Tell Me, whose word is greater?" I had to repent. My faith didn't include praising God for His promise before it was fulfilled.

We often become defeated and discouraged even though we have God's guarantee of victory and success. Abraham was strong in faith and gave glory to God before Sarah conceived, because he had the promise of God.

The final key to Abraham's faith was **being fully persuaded that, what he had promised, he was able also to perform** (4:21). How big is your God? Is your God able? Many times God is too small for our problems, because He is the product of our imaginations.

The God of the Scriptures is eternal and almighty. He measures the heavens with the span of His hand, and to Him "the nations are as a drop of a bucket, and are counted as the small dust of the balance" (Isaiah 40:12, 15). Oh, the greatness of the God we serve! "Now unto him that is able to do exceeding abundantly above all that we ask or think"

(Ephesians 3:20a). Abraham simply believed that God would fulfill His promises, **and therefore it [his faith] was imputed [credited] to him for righteousness** (4:22).

Now it was not written for his sake alone, that it was imputed to him; but for us also, to whom it shall be imputed, if we believe on him that raised up Jesus our Lord from the dead; who was delivered for our offences, and was raised again for our justification (4:23-25).

CHAPTER 5
JUST AS IF I NEVER DID IT

Therefore being justified by faith, we have peace with God (5:1a). "Justified" means "just as if I never did it." The first result of justification by faith is peace with God. If justification depended on my works, some days this peace would be present and some days not, depending on my performance.

We have peace with God through our Lord Jesus Christ: by whom also we have access by faith into this grace wherein we stand (5:1b-2a). The second result of justification by faith is access to God. The door is always open. If we were righteous by our works, then the door would usually be closed because of our failures. Our relationship with God is established on His faithfulness to His promises and on our belief that He'll keep His word.

Satan has bound up many people by accusing them of a lack of righteousness by works. When we begin to pray for a need, he comes and says, "A fine one you are! You pray when you're in trouble, but where were you all week when things were going well? You ought to be ashamed of yourself. God isn't going to listen!" Satan troubles us constantly by claiming that the door is closed. "God doesn't want you to come. You failed to be righteous."

However, my righteousness isn't based on keeping laws but on my belief in Jesus Christ. The door is never closed, even after I've been a miserable failure. I come to Him

through the righteousness given me by faith in Jesus
Christ, and I can be confident of my standing with God.

And [we] rejoice in hope of the glory of God
(5:2b). God's glory will be revealed in my life, and I
rejoice in that!

**And not only so, but we glory in tribulations
also** (5:3a). This verse defines real spiritual growth.
To rejoice in the hope of His glory is much easier than
rejoicing in tribulations. Can I be glad even in hardship? Yes, when I know that my life is governed by
God and that this hardship is producing patience, one
of the greatest needs in my life. "Ye have need of patience, that, after ye have done the will of God, ye
might receive the promise" (Hebrews 10:36).

I've heard people advise others against praying for
patience because God will then send them tribulations. If
that's the way patience comes then I pray, "God, bring on
the troubles." I need patience!

Difficult times cause me to seek God. When all is
well, I don't always respond to Him immediately; but
when I'm in trouble, I want God now. David prayed
much the same way when he was in difficulty. "Answer me speedily" (Psalm 102:2b).

**Tribulation worketh patience; and patience, ex-
perience; and experience, hope** (5:3b-4). In my difficulty I begin to realize that God will provide relief, perhaps not as soon as I'd like, but in His time. Thus, the
experience of trusting in Him during tribulation produces
hope within me.

**And hope maketh not ashamed; because the love
of God is shed abroad in our hearts by the Holy
Ghost which is given unto us. For when we were
yet without strength, in due time Christ died for
the ungodly** (5:5-6). It's important for us to note our

condition when God loved us and allowed His Son to die for us, "the ungodly." We find it difficult to get away from the idea that we must be good so God will love us. God's love for us stems from His nature, not our lovableness.

For scarcely for a righteous man will one die: yet peradventure [perhaps] for a good man some would even dare to die. But God commendeth [demonstrates] his love toward us, in that, while we were yet sinners, Christ died for us (5:7-8). If Christ had died only for good people, we could understand His dying for them. However, Jesus didn't die for the honorable and upright. He died for the ungodly and sinners. By this act God displayed His unconditional love for us.

Much more then, being now justified by his blood, we shall be saved from wrath through him (5:9). If Christ died for us while we were still sinners in rebellion against God, how much more is He willing to save us from the wrath to come?

For if, when we were enemies, we were reconciled to God by the death of his Son, much more, being reconciled, we shall be saved by his life (5:10). These "much mores" are wonderful. While still an enemy of God I was reconciled to Him through the blood of Jesus Christ. If His death could reconcile me as an enemy, how much more will His life establish this loving relationship between God and me.

And not only so, but we also joy in God through our Lord Jesus Christ, by whom we have now received the atonement (5:11). The Old and New Testament words translated "atonement" differ in meaning. Atonement in Hebrew is "kaphar", which means "covering." The Old Testament sacrifices of goats and bulls covered sin but didn't put away sin. The Greek New Testament word for atonement, "katallage", literally means "making one" and would be better translated "rec-

onciliation." Becoming one with God was impossible
through the Old Testament sacrifices; it took the sacrifice of Jesus Christ to reconcile man with God.

**Wherefore, as by one man sin entered into the
world, and death by sin; and so death passed upon
all men, for that all have sinned** (5:12). The word
"have" is added in the King James Version; the origi-
nal Greek reads, "...because all sinned." Paul is saying
that when Adam sinned, he sinned for the whole human race. Just as Adam became a sinful creature, spiritually dead and separated from God, so did his children. Adam couldn't pass along any fellowship with
God to his children, because he had lost it; and because he acted as our federal head, we came into this
world separated from God.

**(For until the law sin was in the world: but sin is
not imputed when there is no law** (5 13). Though sin
was in the world before Moses gave the Law, it wasn't
imputed to men until then.

**Nevertheless death reigned from Adam to Moses,
even over them that had not sinned after the si-
militude of Adam's transgression, who is the figure
of him that was to come** (5:14). Physical death came
as the result of spiritual death. Though God wasn't im-
puting sin to men before the Law, sin was present through
Adam. Death reigned because he sinned for us all.

A dangerous doctrine taught by Jehovah's Witnesses
and other groups is that Adam only sinned for himself.
This view takes away the truth that Paul brings out:
since by one man's sin all could be made sinners, then by
one man's righteousness all can be made righteous (see
Romans 5:19). This corollary is the basis of the doctrine
of justification by faith. One man can act for an entire
body of people, as Adam acted for the entire human race
when he sinned. Even so the second Adam, Jesus Christ,

acted for all of us in His righteousness. It is imputed to all of us who believe in Him. If one man couldn't have sinned for all, then one man couldn't be righteous for all. If that were the case, we would have to establish our own righteousness. That would leave us out in the cold, because "our righteous acts are as filthy rags" in the eyes of God (Isaiah 64:6).

The doctrine that sin passed upon all of us by one man, Adam, is vitally important. I continually warn against the pernicious heresy that says a man is a sinner because he has sinned. Such a concept implies that a man could possibly live and die without sinning. Thus, he wouldn't need Christ. The biblical revelation teaches that a man has sinned because he is a sinner. "By one man sin entered into the world, and death by sin; and so death passed upon all men, for that all have sinned" (5:12).

But not as the offence, so also is the free gift. For if through the offence of one many be dead, much more the grace of God, and the gift by grace, which is by one man, Jesus Christ, hath abounded unto many (5:15). If one man can make us guilty before God, then how much more can Jesus Christ through God's grace make us righteous.

And not as it was by one that sinned, so is the gift: for the judgment was by one to condemnation, but the free gift is of many offences unto justification. For if by one man's offence death reigned by one; much more they which receive abundance of grace and of the gift of righteousness shall reign in life by one, Jesus Christ) (5:16-17). Death reigned from Adam. Life reigns from Christ. If one man can cause the world to die, then how much more can the triumph of Jesus over death bring life to those in Him. "And whosoever liveth and believeth in me shall never die. Believest thou this?" (John 11:26).

Therefore as by the offence of one judgment came upon all men to condemnation; even so by the righteousness of one the free gift came upon all men unto justification of life (5:18). Adam's sin brought condemnation to all men. Christ's sacrifice brought justification to all who believe.

For as by one man's disobedience many were made sinners, so by the obedience of one shall many be made righteous. Moreover the law entered, that the offence might abound. But where sin abounded, grace did much more abound: that as sin hath reigned unto death, even so might grace reign through righteousness unto eternal life by Jesus Christ our Lord (5:19-21).

Thank God for the abounding grace! One version translates verse 20 as "Where sin did abound, grace overflowed." We seem to have great difficulty accepting the grace of God. We're always trying to give God a reason to love us, accept us, or forgive us. But God loves, accepts, and forgives those who are miserable, rotten, and without merit. All we must do is cast ourselves upon Him and cry, "God, be merciful to me a sinner." To him who does not work but simply believes, God imputes his faith for righteousness (Romans 4:5). God accounts me just as righteous as His own dear Son.

CHAPTER 6
VICTORY OVER SIN

What shall we say then? Shall we continue in sin, that grace may abound? (6:1). Since grace overflows wherever sin abounds, should we live in sin so we might see more of the abounding grace of God? Perish the thought!

God forbid. How shall we, that are dead to sin, live any longer therein? (6:2). Here Paul states a fundamental principle about our walk with Christ. The new life in Christ has brought death to the old. "If any man be in Christ, he is a new creature: old things are passed away; behold, all things are become new" (2 Corinthians 5:17). We're dead to sin so we might be alive to God through the Spirit. How can a Spirit-filled being live any longer in sin?

Know ye not, that so many of us as were baptized into Jesus Christ were baptized into his death? Therefore we are buried with him by baptism into death: that like as Christ was raised up from the dead by the glory of the Father, even so we also should walk in newness of life (6:34). When you went down in the waters of baptism, you were actually buried with Christ. As you came up from the waters, you were a new creature—ruled no longer by the flesh but by the Spirit.

For if we have been planted together in the likeness of his death, we shall be also in the likeness of

**his resurrection: knowing this, that our old man
was crucified [past tense in the Greek] with him,
that the body of sin might be destroyed, that hence-
forth we should not serve sin** (6:5-6). The word translated "destroyed" means "put out of business." My body of
sin has been put out of business! If I want forgiveness for
my sins, I must see Christ on the cross dying for me. If I
want power over sin in my life, I must see myself crucified and risen again with Him.

Paul said, "I am crucified with Christ: nevertheless I
live; yet not I, but Christ liveth in me" (Galatians 2:20a).
Your old flesh-dominated nature was crucified, died, and
was buried with Christ. Now you're living after the Spirit-
dominated life. As a child of God, you cannot serve sin
and follow after the weakness of your flesh. God has
freed you from its tyranny, and you need to reckon your
old nature as dead.

**For he that is dead is freed from sin. Now if we
be dead with Christ, we believe that we shall also
live with him: knowing that Christ being raised
from the dead dieth no more; death hath no more
dominion over him. For in that he died, he died
unto sin once: but in that he liveth, he liveth unto
God. Likewise reckon ye also yourselves to be dead
indeed unto sin, but alive unto God through Jesus
Christ our Lord** (6:7-11).

We're to reckon ourselves to be dead unto sin. The
word "reckon" means "to account." This accounting is a
position of faith. As long as we're in this body of flesh, we
have to deal with our flesh which desires to rule over us.
Our old nature was crucified with Christ, and we constantly have to assert this position of faith. Crucifixion is
a slow and tortuous death, as the flesh doesn't die easily.
So, the two positions of faith we must take are that the

old sinful nature is dead and that we're now spiritually alive unto God through Christ.

Let not sin therefore reign in your mortal body, that ye should obey it in the lusts thereof (6:12). Man is an inferior trinity made of body, soul, and spirit. These are set in a vertical order. In the natural man the body is on top, dominating the soul (mind), and the spirit lies underneath, dead, because it's alienated from God. When a man becomes born again by the Spirit of God, his spirit becomes alive and takes reign over the soul, and the desires of the body yield to the spirit. The true child of God is no longer ruled by his flesh.

Neither yield ye your members as instruments [tools or weapons] of unrighteousness unto sin: but yield yourselves unto God, as those that are alive from the dead, and your members as instruments of righteousness unto God (6:13). You have the option of serving the flesh or the Spirit. As a child of God you must yield to the influences of the Spirit and allow your body to be an instrument in God's hands. Don't let the flesh reign over you anymore.

For sin shall not have dominion over you: for ye are not under the law, but under grace (6:14). Grace is the basis of your new relationship with God, and sin does not and cannot have dominion over you.

What then? shall we sin, because we are not under the law, but under grace? God forbid. Know ye not, that to whom ye yield yourselves servants to obey, his servants ye are to whom ye obey; whether of sin unto death, or of obedience unto righteousness? (6:15-16). If you yield to the lust of the flesh, you cannot be a servant of God. You'll become enslaved by your flesh, and it will rule your life, eventually destroying you.

When Adam yielded to temptation and ate of the forbidden fruit, he obeyed Satan's suggestion and became his servant. No man can serve two masters. We cannot serve God and mammon (Matthew 6:24). As we walk in obedience to God, we become the servants of God.

But God be thanked, that ye were the servants of sin, but ye have obeyed from the heart that form of doctrine which was delivered you. Being then made free from sin, ye became the servants of righteousness (6:17-18). We were once the servants of sin, but now we're the servants of God.

I speak, Paul said, **after the manner of men because of the infirmity of your flesh: for as ye have yielded your members servants to uncleanness and to iniquity unto iniquity; even so now yield your members servants to righteousness unto holiness** (6:19).

Again, we face the choice. We must make a willful and deliberate decision not to conform to this world but rather to yield to the Spirit of God. We must reckon the old man to be dead. Christ has set us free. That freedom marks the difference between us and the world. The unbeliever yields to the flesh, because he has no choice. He's under sin's power and has no control over it. Many sinners hate their sins and would like to be set free. Some of them even go to clinics for help. Though their sins gave pleasure for a time, these sins are now ruling and destroying their lives. In contrast, the Christian has been set free from the bondage of corruption. He has come to Jesus Christ in faith and yielded his body as an instrument of God to be controlled by His Spirit.

For when ye were the servants of sin, ye were free from righteousness. What fruit had ye then in those things whereof ye are now ashamed? for

the end of those things is death (6:20-21). The way of the flesh is the path of death.

But now being made free from sin, and become servants to God, ye have your fruit unto holiness, and the end everlasting life. For the wages of sin is death; but the gift of God is eternal life through Jesus Christ our Lord (6:22-23). In a later chapter Paul asks, "What shall we then say to these things? If God be for us, who can be against us?" (Romans 8:31). What "things"? The blessings of eternal life in Christ, God's glorious gift, spoken of here in Chapter 6.

Paul also said, "Not that we are sufficient of ourselves to think any thing as of ourselves; but our sufficiency is of God" (II Corinthians 3:5). God's work in my life is sufficient to bring me to victory. Whenever the flesh rises up and seeks to draw me away, I reckon the old man to be dead, yield my body to God in faith, and receive victory.

Death, sin, and the flesh are always related. To live after the flesh is to miss God's mark for your life. Even so, spirit, righteousness, and life are related. The right God-ordained order for your life is to live after the spirit.

God is a superior Trinity of Father, Son, and Spirit. Man is an inferior trinity of spirit, soul (mind), and body (flesh). If a man's spirit is alive and uppermost, he has fellowship with God. If a man's flesh is uppermost, his fellowship with God is broken, because God wants nothing to do with his sinful flesh. Man can only meet God in the spirit. "God is a Spirit: and they that worship him must worship him in spirit and in truth" (John 4:24). "The Spirit itself beareth witness with our spirit" (Romans 8:16).

CHAPTER 7
FLESH VS. SPIRIT

Here in Chapter 7 we see Paul's agony over trying to personally apply the truths of the previous chapters. A man may know the truth, but its application can cause intense problems.

Paul addresses the opening verses to Jewish believers, not to the general body of Gentile believers. **Know ye not, brethren, (for I speak to them that know the law,) how that the law hath dominion over a man as long as he liveth?** (7:1). The point here is that the Mosaic Law held power over a Jew as long as he lived.

For the woman which hath an husband is bound by the law to her husband so long as he liveth; but if the husband be dead, she is loosed from the law of her husband. So then if, while her husband liveth, she be married to another man, she shall be called an adulteress: but if her husband be dead, she is free from that law; so that she is no adulteress, though she be married to another man. Wherefore, my brethren, ye also are become dead to the law by the body of Christ; that ye should be married to another, even to him who is raised from the dead, that we should bring forth fruit unto God (7:24).

A married woman was bound to her husband as long as he lived or until he divorced her. (In Judaism a woman had no right to divorce her husband. The bride's father would demand a substantial dowry before the marriage

to support the woman in case the husband put her away.
This was actually alimony in advance.)

Gentiles have never been under the Mosaic Law. Even
the early Church fathers decided not to impose the bondage of the Law upon the Gentile believers, since they
weren't able to bear it themselves (Acts 15:13-24).

Paul is showing the Jewish believers that death brought
freedom from the Law and as Christians they had died
with Christ. Therefore, the Jewish believers were set free
from the Law. They had been freed from the Old Covenant by death and joined to the New Covenant through
Jesus Christ.

**For when we were in the flesh, the motions [pas-
sions] of sins, which were by the law, did work in
our members to bring forth fruit unto death. But
now we are delivered from the law, that being dead
wherein we were held; that we should serve in newness of spirit, and not in the oldness of the letter**
(7:5-6). The Law worked in a man's body to bring forth
fruit leading to death. Now he has been delivered from
the Law and a New Covenant has been established. The
Law was never intended to make a man righteous, for if
righteousness could come by the Law then Christ died in
vain (Galatians 2:21). God gave the Law to show man his
sin and to condemn him. It exposes the guilt of the whole
world by revealing man's failure to meet God's standards.

Paul goes on to tell us, **What shall we say then? Is
the law sin? God forbid. Nay, I had not known sin,
but by the law: for I had not known lust [was a
sin], except the law had said, Thou shalt not covet.
But sin, taking occasion by the commandment,
wrought in me all manner of concupiscence. For
without the law sin was dead** (7:7-8). In a tragic misinterpretation of the Law, the Jews had tried to keep it
as their claim to righteousness. This error persists in

Judaism to this day. The modern Jew tries to outweigh his evil deeds with good ones. Yom Kippur, the Day of Atonement, is now a day to reflect over his past actions. However, there's no sacrifice to cover or put away his sin and guilt.

The Law isn't sin, but it certainly brings a man to the awareness of sin. Paul said that he didn't know what sin was until the Law revealed it to him, for without the Law sin was dead.

For I was alive without the law once: but when the commandment came, sin revived, and I died. And the commandment, which was ordained to life, I found to be unto death. For sin, taking occasion by the commandment, deceived me, and by it slew me. Wherefore the law is holy, and the commandment holy, and just, and good. Was then that which is good made death unto me? God forbid. But sin, that it might appear sin, working death in me by that which is good; that sin by the commandment might become exceeding sinful. For we know that the law is spiritual: but I am carnal, sold under sin (7:9-14).

The problem is me. I agree that I should obey the Law. I should love the Lord my God with all my heart, soul, mind, and strength. I should love my neighbor as myself and shouldn't break any of the commandments. The Law is good, right, and just. But with the Law comes the consciousness of God's requirement, and I become aware of how far short I have fallen.

Paul said, "The law is spiritual" (7:14a). By interpreting the Law in a physical sense, the Pharisees believed that they had attained righteousness. As a Pharisee, Paul was blameless in keeping the Law's outward observances. However, when he came to the realization that the Law was spiritual, he stood condemned. He had violated the spirit of the Law many times. The Law, intended to govern the attitudes of men, showed that all were guilty before God. "There is none righteous, no, not one" (Romans 3:10).

Now we need help! The Law brings us to a point of despair and hopelessness. It forces us to look for help beyond ourselves. Any religious system teaching that help can be found within us is bound to fail. Our nature is sinful, in rebellion to God, and not subject to His will. The weakness of the Law isn't in the Law. It is in us.

The first covenant that God established with man was based on rules "which if a man do, he shall live in them" (Leviticus 18:5b). However, man was so sinful that this Old Covenant broke down. So, God established a second covenant with man, the New Covenant based not on keeping rules but on believing in His Son.

Jesus took upon Himself all your guilt and died in your place. For believing in Him, God credits you with the righteousness of Christ. This New Covenant differs diametrically from the old one. The Law depended upon man's faithfulness, and it failed because man was unfaithful. The New Covenant depends upon God's faithfulness, and it stands because God is totally faithful. So, you stand by the grace of God!

For we know that the law is spiritual: but I am carnal, sold under sin. For that which I do I allow [know] not: for what I would, that do I not; but what I hate, that do I (7:14-15). When Paul first realized that the Law was spiritual, he began trying to fulfill the spirit of the Law in his own strength.

Many Christians still try to establish a legal relationship with God. I struggled with this problem for years, because I grew up in a "holiness church". We were always pledging to do good works for God. We'd never smoke, drink, or go to the movies. Our rules weren't the Ten Commandments as such, but regulations set up by our church leaders emphasizing a legal relationship with God.

However, God doesn't want a legal relationship with us. He wants a love relationship. Legal contracts are impersonal and formal, but God wants a love that cannot come by the Law. Paul discovered this truth when he came to the knowledge of Jesus Christ, but he still struggled with his instincts from the old experience. He said, "The things that I really want to do, I don't do; and the things that I don't want to do, I do. And I hate it!"

If then I do that which I would not, I consent unto the law that it is good. Now then it is no more I that do it, but sin that dwelleth in me (7:16-17). The desire to sin isn't the new me, it's my old sinful nature. "For the flesh lusteth against the Spirit, and the Spirit against the flesh: and these are contrary the one to the other: so that ye cannot do the things that ye would" (Galatians 5:17). The non-Christian lives after his flesh and has no conflict with it. The Christian's desires have changed, but he's still in his body of flesh. He wants to please God in his flesh and tries to conform it to the will of God. However, he finds himself doing things that he doesn't want to do.

How many times had I promised God, "I'm going to read ten chapters of the Bible and pray one hour every day this week." Yet I didn't do it. I found myself breaking vows and promises to God, because the good that I wanted to do I couldn't do.

Now then it is no more I that do it, but sin that dwelleth in me. For I know that in me (that is, in my flesh,) dwelleth no good thing: for to will is present with me; but how to perform that which is good I find not (7:17-18). It has taken me many years to come to this truth, and I'm not sure that I completely live by it yet. Sometimes I think that there's some good within me, but more and more I agree with Paul: "in my flesh dwells no good thing."

God passes only one sentence upon our flesh: death. He doesn't remodel the "old man," because the old nature is beyond repair. God has condemned the life of the flesh to death on the Cross.

The will to do good is present within me, but that's not the problem. The problem is my performance. Remember Jesus' words when He came to Peter and found him sleeping: "Could you not watch with me one hour?... The spirit indeed is willing, but the flesh is weak" (Matthew 26:40b, 41b).

For the good that I would I do not: but the evil which I would not, that I do. Now if I do that I would not, it is no more I that do it, but sin that dwelleth in me. I find then a law, that, when I would do good, evil is present with me. For I delight in the law of God after the inward man (7:19-22). Inwardly I consent to obey the Law of God and delight in it. "Lord, I want communion and fellowship with You. I want to be Yours completely."

But I see another law in my members [body], warring against the law of my mind, and bringing me into captivity to the law of sin which is in my members (7:23). This is a real spiritual conflict. "For we wrestle not against flesh and blood, but against principalities," against those strong forces working within our flesh (Ephesians 6:12a).

O wretched man that I am! who shall deliver me from the body of this death? (7:24). You struggle, you try to overcome, you fight against the lusts of the flesh. But you're not making any progress!

As a possible example, let's say that you're overweight. You try every diet that exists. You admit that dieting is good. "I want to get rid of these extra twenty pounds. I'm not going to eat any more hot fudge sundaes." But by next Saturday you can't resist. "The good that I would I do not" (7:19). This body of flesh is still in opposition to your own will, continuing to bring areas of your life into captivity. If this wasn't the case, you would weigh twenty pounds less.

All Christians experience the battle of flesh against spirit. We're chained to a dead man, and wherever we go we drag this old carcass with us. It's smelly, corrupt, and we hate it, yet we're bound to it. In the next chapter of Romans Paul says that we "groan within ourselves, waiting for the adoption, to wit, the redemption of our body" (Romans 8:23b). Oh, how we long to live in a redeemed body! Then we won't have this struggle anymore.

At this point in his walk Paul was struggling with the desires of the body. He found that his flesh brought him into captivity, and he was acting in ways that he didn't want to. There was great conflict between his will and actions, between his spirit and flesh. In desperation he finally cried out, "Who shall deliver me?" When we cry out like this, help is near.

The highly effective Alcoholics Anonymous program recognizes and teaches this principle. First, the member must recognize that he has a problem. Second, he must seek help beyond himself. This is the key for real deliverance.

I'm living in this body of the flesh which has a tremendous influence on me. However, I can't overcome its power by myself. "Who shall deliver me?" By reaching out and taking hold of God, I begin to experience the overcoming power of His Spirit. Now I find that God can do what I can't do for myself.

As long as you're trying to deliver yourself, the Christian life will be one frustration and defeat after another. **With the mind I myself serve the law of God; but with the flesh the law of sin** (7:25b). You want to do good and serve God, yet you're overcome by the impulses and desires of the flesh. As long as you're striving on your own, you'll find yourself living in the anguish described in Chapter 7 of Romans.

In despair I cry out for help. "Who shall deliver me from the body of this death?" Paul said, **I thank God through Jesus Christ our Lord** (7:25a). Must I forever struggle, fight, and be defeated by my flesh? No. Through Jesus Christ our Lord, God has given me a way out. I don't have to be overcome by my fleshly nature anymore, for in Him I find true deliverance.

CHAPTER 8
SET FREE!

In Chapter 8 Paul explains how God looks upon the mind and heart of the Christian who desires to serve and follow after Him. God sees his faith in Jesus Christ, and **There is therefore now no condemnation to them who are in Christ Jesus, who walk not after the flesh, but after the Spirit. For the law of the Spirit of life in Christ Jesus hath made me free from the law of sin and death** (8:1-2).

For years mankind was under the law of sin and death. When we would want to do good, evil was present. We were bound by sin and death just as we're bound by the law of gravity. It was holding us earthbound or, more accurately, flesh-bound.

However, the law of gravity can be overcome by the proper application of certain natural laws, such as the principle of aerodynamics. Though aerodynamics doesn't negate gravity, it can overcome its force. Likewise, the application of certain spiritual laws can overcome the law of sin and death.

I'm no longer condemned by the Law of Moses, because the new law of faith operates in my life. I enter this new relationship with God through Jesus Christ and experience the life of Christ, which sets me free from the old Law. This new law of faith in Christ overcomes the effects of the old Law of condemnation.

For what the law could not do, in that it was weak through the flesh, God sending his own Son in the

**likeness of sinful flesh, and for sin, condemned sin in
the flesh** (8:3). The Mosaic Law couldn't make me righteous,
because my sinful nature prevented true obedience.

In contrast, this new law of life makes me righteous before
God. **That the righteousness of the law might be fulfilled in us, not by us** (8:4a). I no longer try to attain my
righteousness by observing the Law of Moses. The Law and
its righteousness is fulfilled in me, because Jesus Christ has
fulfilled it for me.

Who walk not after the flesh, but after the Spirit
(8:4b). The requirements for fulfilling the righteousness of
the Law are met by living according to the Spirit and not
walking after the flesh.

**For they that are after the flesh do mind the
things of the flesh; but they that are after the Spirit
the things of the Spirit. For to be carnally minded
is death; but to be spiritually minded is life and
peace** (8:5-6). Since I'm walking after the Spirit, I now
live according to the things of the Spirit. With this spiri-
tual-mindedness I have life and peace.

The two main parts of man's nature are flesh and spirit.
He also possesses a consciousness, his mind, which is controlled by either his body or spirit. If he walks after the flesh,
his mind is controlled by the flesh; if he walks after the
Spirit, it's controlled by the Spirit.

When God created Adam, He formed the body from the
dust of the earth. At first Adam's body had no life. Then God
breathed into that figure "and man became a living soul"
(Genesis 2:7c), a trinity of spirit, mind, and body.

Because God's breath was in him, man became a spiritual creature with a consciousness governed by God. Since
Adam had the mind of the Spirit, he walked and com-
muned with God in the Garden of Eden. Though he had
his bodily appetites, he wasn't ruled by them. When he

disobeyed God and obeyed the lust of his flesh by eating the forbidden fruit, his nature was turned around. Its order became body, soul, and spirit. The flesh took control of his mind, and he lost the consciousness of fellowship with God. Coming to the Garden to commune with him, God cried, "Adam, where are you?" Adam was hiding because he had alienated himself from God.

Even today, every man dominated by his body is alienated from God and the life of God. The mind of the flesh is death (8:6), and such a mind has no awareness of the presence or love of God. It is dead to God and the things of the Spirit.

Jesus said, "Whatever is born of flesh is flesh. To be born of the Spirit, you must be born again" (John 3:3, 6). When I'm born again, the old things pass away and all things become new. Conversion takes place by the Spirit of God, and I become as new as when God created Adam.

The order of my nature is now spirit, soul, and body, the order that God intended for man. I begin to have the mind of the Spirit, which is life. The awareness of God's presence pervades my life and I desire more of Him and the things of God. Peace with God, peace within myself, and peace with my brothers now fills me, because God has brought me back to life.

For they that are after the flesh do mind the things of the flesh (8:5a). Jesus described the people of the world as always concerned with eating, drinking, and clothing themselves. "What shall we eat? What shall we drink? What shall we wear?" (Matthew 6:31).

But they that are after the Spirit do mind [have their minds set on] the things of the Spirit (8:5b). Those who are born again are absorbed with the ways of God, His love, and His Word. They seek Him first.

For to be carnally minded is death; but to be spiritually minded is life and peace. Because the carnal

mind is enmity against God: for it is not subject to the law of God, neither indeed can be. So then they that are in the flesh cannot please God (8:6-8). The carnal mind brings death, because it's in a losing war with God. The mind of the flesh doesn't yield to God's Law, since it's in rebellion. Thus it cannot please God.

But ye are not in the flesh, but in the Spirit, if so be that the Spirit of God dwells in you. Now if any man have not the Spirit of Christ, he is none of his. And if Christ be in you, the body is dead because of sin; but the Spirit is life because of righteousness (8:9-10). We find the delivering power of the Spirit through the indwelling of Jesus Christ. What we cannot do for ourselves He does for us.

Bob Munger wrote a wonderful booklet, "My Heart Christ's Home" (Inter Varsity Press, 1954). In it he describes a Christian who invites Christ to come in, settle down, and make Himself at home in his heart. The day this fellow invited Christ into his heart was glorious. Every morning the Lord and he would rise early, sit together, plan the day, and talk in beautiful, warm fellowship. As the days went by, the Christian gradually began getting up too late to enjoy this fellowship. Seeing Jesus sitting and waiting for him, he'd say, "Lord, I'm in a hurry today. But I'll be back tomorrow." Then he'd rush out the door.

After many days passed, the man longed for real fellowship with the Lord. Early one morning he stopped by, sat down, and said, "Oh, Lord, I've missed this!" He was surprised to hear Him say, "I've missed it, too."

One day the Christian came home from work and the Lord said, "There's a horrible smell in this house. I located it in the closet upstairs, but the closet door is locked."

The man said, "I've given You the whole house. All I've kept for myself is that little closet upstairs. Why can't You just ignore it?"

"I can't live in the same house with that smell," Jesus said. "Either it goes or I go."

The man softened. "Actually, I've tried to clean that up for a long time, but I don't think I can, Lord."

The Lord said, "Will you give me the permission to clean it up for you? Just give me the key, and I'll take care of it."

The man reluctantly handed over the key. The Lord went to work. He cleaned and scrubbed until He got rid of the stink and filth in that closet. Though the Christian was unable to do the job himself, he discovered that the Lord would do it, if only he would yield. After the work was done, fellowship between the two was better than ever.

Maybe you have a locked closet in your heart. The Lord is saying, "This area of the flesh that you still serve must go." Simply give Him the key. He'll do a terrific job of cleaning the mess in that old, smelly closet.

And if Christ be in you, the body [old nature] is dead because of sin; but the Spirit is life because of righteousness. But if the Spirit of him that raised up Jesus from the dead dwell in you, he that raised up Christ from the dead shall also quicken your mortal bodies by his Spirit that dwelleth in you (8:1-11). As Jesus was raised from the dead by the power of the Holy Spirit, we also are made alive by the Holy Spirit. We have a new life, the resurrected life of Christ.

As a Christian, I need to recognize that my old nature was crucified. I'm now living according to my new nature and walking after the Spirit. With the Spirit of God dwelling in me, I'm not following after the flesh but after the Spirit.

Therefore, brethren, we are debtors, not to the flesh, to live after the flesh (8:12). I don't owe my old nature anything, because I've been freed from that bondage.

For if ye live after the flesh, ye shall die: but if ye through the Spirit do mortify the deeds of the body,

ye shall live (8:13). Who will deliver me from the deeds of
the body? God has provided the plan of victory through the
Holy Spirit. The disciples were promised, "You will receive
power when the Holy Spirit comes upon you" (Acts 1:8). He
gives us the power to live as He wants us to live, freeing us
from the bondage of the flesh.

**For as many as are led by the Spirit of God, they
are the sons of God** (8:14). Many people claim to be children of God; but it's not what they claim that counts, it's
what they are (see I John 4:20-21). Do they follow the Spirit
of God, or do they live without seeking His will?

**For ye have not received the spirit of bondage again
to fear; but ye have received the Spirit of adoption,
whereby we cry, Abba, Father. The Spirit itself beareth
witness with our spirit, that we are the children of
God** (8:15-16). Abba is Aramaic for "father." I've been adopted
by God into His family, and His Spirit bears witness with
mine that I'm His son. So, it's only natural for me to cry,
"Father! Father!"

**And if children, then heirs; heirs of God, and
joint-heirs with Christ** (8:17a). God has given Christ
everything because He is the Son. Becoming a child of
God through Jesus Christ makes me a joint-heir of all
things with Him. Jesus said, "Then shall the King say
unto them on his right hand, Come, ye blessed of my
Father, inherit the kingdom prepared for you from the
foundation of the world" (Matthew 25:34). As a child of
God, all the Father owns belongs to me, potentially.

**If so be that we suffer with him, that we may be
also glorified together** (8:17b). When Moses came of
age, the Egyptian throne was his for the taking. He chose
"to suffer affliction with the people of God, [rather] than
to enjoy the pleasures of sin for a season; esteeming the
reproach of Christ greater riches than the treasures in

Egypt: for he had respect unto the recompense of the reward" (Hebrews 11:25-26).

Moses could have been the Pharaoh of Egypt, spending all the years of this life in pomp and glory; or he could choose to suffer with the children of God on earth and spend eternity in the glory of God's kingdom. Moses made a wise decision. He chose the worst that the Lord had to offer, the reproach of Christ, rather than the best the world had to offer, the kingdom of man. If you were to ask him about it today, he'd say, "I made the right choice. For the past 3800 years I've been enjoying its benefits. I have no regrets!"

For enduring the reproach of Christ we'll be glorified together. **For I reckon that the sufferings of this present time are not worthy to be compared with the glory which shall be revealed in us** (8:18). Paul wrote to the Corinthians, "Our light affliction, which is but for a moment, worketh for us a far more exceeding and eternal weight of glory" (II Corinthians 4:17). Notice the contrast between "light affliction" and "eternal weight," affliction for a "moment" and "eternal... glory." Our present sufferings aren't worth comparing with the glory to be revealed.

For the earnest expectation of the creature [creation] waiteth for the manifestation of the sons of God (8:19). Certain egotistic Christians apply this Scripture to their own fellowships, claiming that the world is waiting for their manifestation. I can understand their self-centered feelings. When I graduated from seminary I thought the world was waiting for me, too. After years in school, I was thrilled to get my diploma, receive my assignment, and head out to save the world. I was shocked. Nobody was waiting for me. I had to bribe people to attend church by giving them lollipops. The fact is that the world isn't waiting for any group to be manifested. Besides, Paul isn't talking about such a manifestation here.

Paul explains the meaning. **For the creature [referring to us] was made subject to vanity [emptiness], not willingly, but by reason of him who hath subjected the same in hope** (8:20). For His own reasons God created man with an emptiness. This spiritual void causes man to seek after God, to find Him, and to fellowship with Him. Tragically, man often tries to fill that spiritual void with the things of this world. However, his physical and emotional experiences only lead to a greater sense of emptiness.

As man exists on the three levels of body, soul, and spirit, so his needs create drives on these three levels. We're all too familiar with our bodily drives, such as air, thirst, hunger, bowel and bladder or sex. We also recognize our soulish drives for security, love, the need to be needed, etc. What man so often tries to ignore is the crying need in his spirit for a meaningful relationship with God. As the psalmist David said, "My soul longs after thee, O God" (Psalm 84:2).

As long as you're trying to fill that spiritual void in your life with the things of this world, you'll find that the inner cry for God goes on. The moment you invite Jesus Christ to come and dwell in your spirit, you'll begin to experience the fullness that God desires you to know through Him.

Because the creature itself also shall be delivered from the bondage of corruption into the glorious liberty of the children of God. For we know that the whole creation groaneth and travaileth in pain together until now. And not only they [the world around us], but ourselves also, which have the firstfruits of the Spirit, even we ourselves groan within ourselves, waiting for the adoption, to wit, the redemption of our body (8:21-23).

Paul speaks of bringing the creation into the glorious freedom of the children of God. This doesn't mean that Christians will be manifested as sons of God taking over earthly governments and ushering in God's kingdom of righteousness and peace. Paul is saying that God will exchange my old body for a new one, and I'll be with Him when He returns in power and glory to establish the kingdom of God on earth. I'm waiting for a new body to be in perfect harmony with my redeemed spirit. Then the war against my flesh will finally be over. Oh, how I long for that day!

In I Corinthians 15:51 Paul speaks of a new revelation from God: we will not all sleep as in death, but "we shall all be changed" in a moment. This corruptible body will be changed into an incorruptible one; this mortal body will be exchanged for an immortal one. The greatest problems in my Christian life have come from the weakness of my flesh. Once I experience that glorious metamorphosis, my problems will be over. Even so, come quickly, Lord Jesus.

For we are saved by hope: but hope that is seen is not hope: for what a man seeth, why doth he yet hope for? But if we hope for that we see not, then do we with patience wait for it (8:24-25). If this body of flesh was already perfected and free of all worldly lusts, why would I hope for deliverance? My hope is in God's promise of His future work.

As long as I'm in this body, I'll be subject to its imperfections; but there's no condemnation against me, because I'm walking after the Spirit. I love Christ, and so God doesn't impute my unrighteousness to me. He has accounted me righteous, because with my mind I'm serving the law of the Spirit, even though with my flesh I'm still stumbled and sometimes fall. My failures are painful to me just as they're painful to Him. Thank God that my anxiety will one day be over. Paul says that while we're locked in this body "we groan, earnestly desiring to be clothed upon with our house which is from heaven... that mortality might be swallowed up by life" (II Corinthians 5:2, 4b) . Until the reality of that day, I hope and wait patiently for God to complete His work.

Likewise the Spirit also helpeth our infirmities: for we know not what we should pray for as we ought: but the Spirit itself maketh intercession for us with groanings which cannot be uttered (8:26). One weakness of this body is a lack of knowledge about God's will in every situation. Since the purpose of prayer is to open the doors for God's will to be done, how can I pray when I don't know His will? The Spirit helps me to overcome my ignorance.

Suppose that God is freeing a Christian from his old, natural ways through a series of trials. Seeing the man suffering, I pray, "Lord, deliver him from his trials." However, the worst thing in the world for that man would be deliverance from his trials before the work of God was completed. So, I could be praying in opposition to the will of God in my brother's life.

Enter the Spirit, who "maketh intercession for us with groanings which cannot be uttered." To God the deep, wordless utterances of heartfelt prayer aren't unintelligible sounds, but powerful supplications. God understands them completely, for the Spirit within the believer prays according to the will of God.

Such divine intercession can seemingly insult my intelligence. After all, I want to understand the situation, but these unintelligible groanings affront my natural understanding. However, by faith I pray in the Spirit. For we're told, **He that searcheth the hearts knoweth what is the mind of the Spirit, because he maketh intercession for the saints according to the will of God** (8:27). The Spirit intercedes according to God's will, for God knows "what is the mind of the Spirit." Surely we should talk less and "groan" more!

And we know that all things work together for good (8:28a). A variation of this Scripture has become popular in many Christian circles: "We know that some things work together for good." They think that God has a purpose for some things, but not all things. "Why did God allow me to go through that difficult experience? What possible good can come from that?" Yet God's Word remains true and unchanging.

For whom do all things work together for good? For every man and woman on the street? No. **To them that love God, to them who are the called according to his purpose** (8:28b). Only a child of God can have this wonderful assurance.

Romans 8:28 has sustained me through some of the most difficult experiences of my life. When everything comes apart and I don't understand the events around me, I fall back on this verse. "All things work together for good..." God has a good purpose for everything I experience, because I love Him and He has called me according to His plan. This gives me peace in chaotic circumstances and strength in the hour of great testing. How this buoys me up when my intellect is exhausted from struggling to understand. What blessed assurance for the saints of God!

For whom he did foreknow, he also did predestinate to be conformed to the image of his Son, that he might be the firstborn among many brethren (8:29). A subject such as predestination can create quite a problem within the Church. The difficulty usually arises from extending a truth of God to a seemingly logical conclusion.

The problem about predestination can be stated like this: "If God has already predestined those who are saved, then He must have also predestined those who are lost. In that case, why should we do anything to save the lost? Those predestined to be saved surely will be saved. And there's nothing we can do about those who are predestined to be lost. So, why worry about it? Why witness? Why support missionaries? Why pray?" How far astray human reasoning can go on a simple truth of God.

You must have all the facts about a case in order to make a reasoned judgment, but you don't and can't know all the facts about predestination. "For whom he did foreknow..." Do you have foreknowledge?

God knew in advance who would respond to His love and grace, and these He predestined to be conformed to the image of His Son. The example of a football game rerun might be helpful in understanding this concept. If you saw the game in person, you already know what happened. You won't get excited watching the rerun on TV, even in the tension-packed closing minutes. You know which team won.

In the Psalms Moses declared that our lives are spent as a tale that is told (Psalm 90:9b). From God's point of view our lives are like a rerun. He knows in advance every decision, response, and reaction we'll make. So, I don't understand God's predestination because I don't look at life as He does. I don't know the end from the beginning, for I only "see through a glass darkly" (I Corinthians 13:12).

The difficulty lies in trying to understand how an omnipotent God makes His choices. I hear people say that His choices aren't fair. But what do they know about it? Nothing! The ways of the Lord are beyond man's understanding, and His mind is far beyond man's ability to comprehend (Romans 11:34).

Of course I believe in predestination, since it's plainly taught in the Scriptures. The doctrine could be assumed, even if the word was never explicitly used. It's a thrilling truth that doesn't upset me at all. The fact that He chose me and began a good work in me proves that He'll continue to perform it. He wouldn't bring me this far and then dump me.

When did God choose me? When I surrendered my life to Jesus? No. When I decided to serve Him? No. When He saw that He could do some work in me? No. God chose me before He ever formed the foundations of this world (Ephesians 1:4). He established the glorious plan for my life millenniums ago.

My future with Him is as good as accomplished, because He knows it'll be worked out perfectly.

Moreover whom he did predestinate, them he also called: and whom he called, them he also justified: and whom he justified, them he also glorified (8:30). This verse takes me from the past to the future, showing God's complete work of predestination, calling, justification, and glorification. Although my glorification is yet to come, God speaks of it as past history. What glorious assurance is mine in Christ Jesus. God—who speaks of things before they are as though they were, because He knows all things and knows they shall be, and as far as He is concerned they are already—has spoken of my glorification. It's as certain as His Word.

What shall we then say to these things? (8:31a). I say, "Hallelujah!" I love the wonderful truth of what God has done for me.

If God be for us, who can be against us? (8:31b). God is for you. He's planned your journey through life from the beginning of the ages, and now He's working it out before your eyes.

During the early years of my Christian experience, I thought that God was against me. I imagined that He was making a list and checking it twice, and He would punish me because I hadn't been very nice. God was waiting for me to make a mistake, so He could order me out of the game. I was terrified. O what joy I found when I learned that God was for me! I rejoice because He has made all the powers of heaven to strengthen and sustain me, not to destroy me. The powers of God are working for me, and they're much greater and stronger than the powers that are working against me.

If God is for me, who can be against me? Satan can, but who is he compared to God? He isn't on an equal level with God. We sometimes think of him as God's opposite, but he isn't. As a created being Satan cannot be

compared to God in any area. The vast disparity between
the finite and the infinite defies comparison. More like
the demonic equivalent of an archangel, Satan might
give Michael or Gabriel a bad time (Daniel 10:13-14), but
he's no match for God.

Who can be against me? The world, the flesh, and the
devil are against me. But these are no match for God who
helps me, strengthens me, and works to present me faultless
before His glorious presence with great joy (Jude 24).

**He that spared not his own Son, but delivered him
up for us all, how shall he not with him also freely
give us all things?** (8:32). Here Paul encourages us by
moving from the greater to the lesser. What do you need
from God? "Lord, my needs are so many. How will You ever
supply them?" For starters, look what He's already given
you. The things that you presently need are nothing by comparison. He loves you so much that He spared not His own
Son. You were redeemed not with perishable things such as
silver and gold from the empty life you used to lead, but with
the precious blood of Jesus Christ, who was slain as a lamb
without spot or blemish (I Peter 1:18-19).

**Who shall lay any thing to the charge of God's elect?
It is God that justifieth** (8:33). Is God charging me with
sin? No. "Blessed is the man to whom the Lord does not
impute sin" (Psalm 32:2). However, Satan accuses me day
and night. He charges me with failure, incompetence, and
countless horrible offenses. Yet God has justified me, and He
cannot accuse me and justify me at the same time. So why
should I worry?

Who is he that condemneth? (8:34a). Not God. The
Holy Spirit may be convicting me of sin, but He isn't condemning me. Condemnation is the work of Satan.

What's the difference between the condemnation of Satan and the conviction of the Holy Spirit? When Satan
condemns me, I want to run from God. "You've failed

God so miserably and completely!" Satan says. "You have no right to ask for His help. He's tired of you and your failures. Why don't you do Him a favor and drop dead?" I often find myself agreeing with Satan and becoming alienated from God. His condemnation drives me from God. Whenever I think, "I shouldn't approach God because of what I've done," Satan is condemning me.

When the Spirit convicts me, I can't wait to come to God. The Spirit of God deals with me by drawing me to Him. "Lord, I want to confess this sin!"

"Who is he that condemneth?" Satan condemns me, people often condemn me, and I condemn myself; but none of these count. Jesus is the one who counts, and He is far from condemning me. He intercedes on my behalf.

It is Christ that died, yea rather, that is risen again, who is even at the right hand of God, who also maketh intercession for us (8:34b). Jesus stands before God and says, "Father, there's Chuck. Forgive him for My sake. I paid for all his sins." Jesus never says, "Father, I'm tired of Chuck! Why don't we just shove him out?" Jesus is interceding for me, not condemning me.

Paul now bursts forth with a glorious statement. **Who shall separate us from the love of Christ? shall tribulation, or distress, or persecution, or famine, or nakedness, or peril, or sword? As it is written, For thy sake we are killed all the day long; we are accounted as sheep for the slaughter. Nay, in all these things we are more than conquerors through him that loved us. For I am persuaded, that neither death, nor life, nor angels, nor principalities, nor powers, nor things present, nor things to come, nor height, nor depth, nor any other creature, shall be able to separate us from the love of God, which is in Christ Jesus our Lord** (8:35-39). I'm tied in so tightly to God that nothing can remove me from His love.

> Blessed assurance, Jesus is mine!
> Oh, what a foretaste of glory divine!
> Heir of salvation, purchase of God,
> Born of His Spirit, washed in His blood.
> This is my story, this is my song,
> Praising my Savior all the day long.[1]

God loved me before the foundation of the world. He loved me when I was a wretch who hated Him and rebelled against Him. How much more does He love me now that I'm fumbling, struggling, and seeking to do my best to serve Him. Now my heart is open to Him, my desires are toward Him, and I love Him and want to serve Him. How much more will He sustain me through my weaknesses, strengthen me in my desperate hour, draw me daily to Himself, and grant me His victory within my life. The principalities and powers of darkness cannot overthrow me, because I'm more than a conqueror through Him that loves me. I belong to Jesus now and forever.

I'm sure of my relationship with God and my eternal life in Him. I have nothing to fear or to worry about. I simply cling to my Lord Jesus Christ. He has loved me and I love Him because of His love. He has filled me with His Spirit, given me His power, and strengthened me day by day. Glory to God forever and ever!

---

[1] From Blessed Assurance by Fanny J. Crosby.

CHAPTER 9
CHOSEN

At this point in his letter Paul explains that God has removed the national privileges and blessings from Israel. The Jews had enjoyed a most-favored-nation status with God. However, by rejecting the righteousness provided for them through Jesus the Messiah, the "natural branch" of Israel has been cut off for a time.

In matters of salvation, Israel no longer retains a privileged status. Jew and Gentile alike must come to Jesus, for He is God's answer for every man's sin. "All have sinned, and come short of the glory of God; being justified freely by his grace through the redemption that is in Christ Jesus" (Romans 3:23-24).

As he speaks of Israel's severance from its divine privileges, Paul realizes that many will accuse him of bitterness against the Jews because they rejected him. Lest he be charged with contempt toward his own race, he begins by affirming his love for the Jews, a love as strong as Moses'. "Please forgive their sin," Moses interceded after Israel had made the golden calf. "And if not, blot me, I pray thee, out of thy book which thou hast written" (Exodus 32:32). Like Moses, Paul was willing to give up his own salvation for the sake of his fellow Jews, and with this deep concern he begins his discussion of Israel.

I say the truth in Christ, I lie not, my conscience also bearing me witness in the Holy Ghost, that I have great heaviness and continual sorrow in my heart.

For I could wish that myself were accursed from Christ for my brethren, my kinsmen according to the flesh: who are Israelites (9:1-4a).

Paul's great burden for the Jews weighs heavily upon his heart. He grieves that they're neglecting the righteousness provided by God in Jesus Christ. He grieves, too, that his brothers by heritage have now been cut off from God's fellowship and denied the blessings and favors which were once upon them. He describes these blessings: **to whom pertaineth the adoption, and the glory, and the covenants, and the giving of the law, and the service of God, and the promises** (9:4b). Let's look at these more closely.

First, the Jews had been adopted by God as His own people, because Abraham believed by faith that God would do as He promised. "I will make of thee a great nation" (Genesis 12:2a). God made a nation from Abraham through which the Messiah came. He watched over, cared for, and nurtured the children of Abraham as His own. God's adoption of the Jews eventually included the Gentiles . In thee [Abraham] shall all families of the earth be blessed" (Genesis 12:3b).

Second, the glory of God rested upon Israel. When the Jews left Egypt, the glory of God went with them in the form of a cloud by day and a pillar of fire by night (Exodus 13:22). The consciousness of His presence was constantly with Israel. In the wilderness the glory of God filled the Holy of Holies in the tabernacle (Exodus 29:43), and He dwelt in the midst of His people. The glory of God descended on their place of worship when Solomon built the temple in Jerusalem (I Kings 8:10-11). The glory of God's presence was their privilege.

Third, God had made a covenant with Abraham. He then established that covenant with the nation through the Law of Moses. He would be their God through the giving of the Law, and they would be His people through their service to Him.

Finally, God had made promises to this nation, promises that are still valid. Today, we see the Lord fulfilling His word to His people. He said He would bring the Jews back into their land from all nations (Ezekiel 34:13, 36:24). As the whole world knows, the Jews *are* back in their land. God promised, "Israel shall blossom and bud, and fill the face of the world with fruit" (Isaiah 27:6). Israel is the world's third largest exporter of fruit and does indeed "fill the face of the world with fruit." Exporting flowers is also a major Israeli industry. The country continues to literally "blossom and bud" as God fulfills His word.

Paul goes on to say that to Israel belong **the fathers [patriarchs] and of whom as concerning the flesh Christ came, who is over all, God blessed forever. Amen** (9:5).

There have been several poor translations of this verse by scholars who deny the deity of Jesus Christ. In fact, the Revised Standard Version (RSV) handles the translation so blasphemously that it cannot even be considered an accurate rendering. In Greek verse five reads, "...as concerning the flesh Christ came, who is God over all, blessed forever." Here Paul plainly declares that Christ is God over all. The RSV turns this verse into a doxology, and so removes the force of Paul's declaration of Christ's deity: "...according to the flesh, is the Christ. God who is over all be blessed forever." This interpretation changes the meaning of the text. Paul affirms Christ's deity throughout his Epistles, and this verse is one of his strongest and clearest affirmations.

Not as though the word of God hath taken none effect. For they are not all Israel, which are of Israel (9:6). Not all the descendants of Jacob are truly of Israel. To find out what Paul means, let's look at the story of Jacob in the Old Testament.

Jacob and Esau, the sons of Isaac, were twins, Esau being born first. He looked like a hairy, red garment, so his parents named him Hairy, in Hebrew "Esau." Jacob grabbed his brother's heel during birth, so they named him Heel-catcher, which is "Jacob" in Hebrew (a name that came to mean "deceiver" or "supplanter").

As the oldest son, Esau stood to inherit the birthright. One day, Jacob took advantage of his brother's great hunger and traded Esau a mess of pottage for the birthright. Later, when their father Isaac was to place the family blessing on Esau, Jacob tricked his old, blind father and received the blessing intended for his brother. When Esau discovered that Jacob had cheated him out of his blessing, he threatened to kill him. Afraid, Jacob fled to his uncle who lived far away.

After many years, Jacob decided to return home. He had only traveled partway when he received news that Esau was coming to him with a large company of men. Fear gripped Jacob's heart and he really prayed!

That night an angel of the Lord wrestled with Jacob. When the angel saw that he couldn't prevail against Jacob, he touched his hip and it slipped out of joint. In this crippled condition Jacob cried, "I won't let you go until you bless me!"

"What is your name?" the angel asked.

"Heel-catcher," said Jacob.

The angel replied, "Your name will no longer be Heel-catcher, but Israel" (Genesis 32:2-28). Jacob's new name meant "governed by God." Paul said, "For they are not all Israel, which are of Israel." In other words, not all the descendants of Jacob are governed by God.

In biblical times most names had significance, because the people related them to the personal characteristics of the individual. Paul tells us that no one is truly Israel unless he is governed by God. We have a parallel situation with the word "Christian." Not everyone who is called a Christian is truly a follower of Christ.

Neither, because they are the seed of Abraham, are they all children: but, In Isaac shall thy seed be called (9:7). Ishmael, a son of Abraham who became the father of the Arabs, didn't inherit the promises. So, not all of the descendants of Abraham are God's chosen people.

God promised Abraham a son through Sarah. "I will bless her, and give thee a son also of her" (Genesis 17:16a). However, Abraham wanted God to accept the work of his flesh with Ishmael, so he said, "O that Ishmael might live before thee!" (Genesis 17:18). But God refused to honor Abraham's request.

Ishmael represents the man of the flesh and Isaac the man of the spirit. Ishmael, the result of Abraham's attempt to help God, wasn't recognized, because God doesn't recognize the works of our flesh. God told Abraham, "Take now thy son, thine only son Isaac" (Genesis 22:2a). God didn't even acknowledge Ishmael as Abraham's son.

How often we serve God in the energies of our flesh. Many ministers try building their churches through publicity campaigns, promotions, and financial analysis. They're using the efforts of the flesh to promote God's work.

For example, let's say that we wanted to raise a million dollars for our church. For a ten percent commission, professionals specializing in fund-raising drives for churches will raise the money for us, guaranteed. Many churches use such services.

This is just one tragic testimony of the Church's failure to walk in the Spirit. Following the ways of the world, she tries to do the work of God. But God doesn't want works in the energies and power of the flesh offered to Him. He refuses them. The Church's only hope of survival is to be led and energized by the Spirit of God. The

Church is too big to push with the flesh, and unless the Spirit of God keeps working, she's finished.

God's promises to Abraham greatly affect today's Mideast situation. When Abraham first settled in the land, God said, "Lift up now thine eyes, and look from the place where thou art northward, and southward, and eastward, and westward: for all the land which thou seest, to thee will I give it, and to thy seed forever" (Genesis 13:14-15). This promise wasn't made to Ishmael and his descendants, the Arabs. It was made to the chosen heir, Isaac, and his descendants, the Jews.

That is, They which are the children of the flesh, these are not the children of God: but the children of the promise are counted for the seed. For this is the word of promise, At this time will I come, and Sarah shall have a son. And not only this; but when Rebecca also had conceived by one, even by our father Isaac; (for the children being not yet born, neither having done any good or evil, that the purpose of God according to election might stand, not of works, but of him that calleth;) it was said unto her, The elder shall serve the younger (9:8-12).

As God made a distinction between Isaac and Ishmael, the sons of Abraham, so He distinguished between Jacob and Esau, the sons of Isaac. Jacob was accepted, and through him the promises and the Messiah came. Esau was rejected, and prophecies speak of his descendants being cut off as a nation (Genesis 36:9 with Obadiah 9-10).

As it is written, Jacob have I loved, but Esau have I hated (9:13). This is difficult for us to understand. Why, before Jacob and Esau were ever born, would God accept one and reject the other? The reason is that salvation stands by election alone and not by works. God calls and elects whomever He wishes.

I can't honestly look at myself and say that God elected me because I'm so good. God simply acted on the basis of His own divine sovereignty. The fact that God chose to elect me thrills me and makes me ever grateful to Him.

God chose between Jacob and Esau before they were born. While they were still in the womb, He said, "The elder shall serve the younger" (Genesis 25:23b; Romans 9:12). Of course, God foreknew the attitudes and responses of each son before he was born. God made His choice with the knowledge that Jacob would be a spiritual man and Esau a fleshly one. Yet, no one can say that Jacob was elected because he was so wonderful, kind, or generous. God simply chose him.

What shall we say then? Is there unrighteousness with God? (9:14). Our logical conclusion to this is that God is unfair. However, as we said before, carrying the truths of God to our own logical conclusions is dangerous. There are facts about each case that we don't know or understand, because our knowledge is limited. We cannot reason as God or know all the things He knows.

Is there unrighteousness with God? God forbid (9:14). God does what is right. His selections are perfectly justified. He bestows His love and grace upon whom He wills, and He has the right to do so. Thank God that He chose me!

You may say, "God didn't choose me."

"How do you know you're not chosen?"

"Because I'm not a Christian."

"Why don't you accept Jesus?"

"I don't want to."

Isn't it amazing that you don't want to choose God, yet you want to find fault with Him because He didn't choose you? The only way to know whether or not He chose you is to believe. You'll then discover that He had chosen you before

you were even born. No one has ever called upon the name of
the Lord and been told, "Sorry, your name isn't on the list."

I have some difficulty when God says, "Esau have I hated."
I have even more difficulty when He says, "Jacob have I
loved." Jacob wasn't so lovable.

My greatest difficulty comes when God says that He loves
me. I'm not at all lovable! God's glorious grace is manifested
in His love for any of us—Jacob, me, or you.

"For all have sinned, and come short of the glory of God"
(Romans 3 :23). God would be justified in destroying all men.
If God wiped out the human race, no one could point a finger
of accusation at Him. So why are we accusing God of unfair-
ness when He chooses to redeem some from destruction?

Again, we cannot enter into God's reasoning processes.
God operates on a level far above ours. "For who hath
known the mind of the Lord? or who hath been his counsellor?" (Isaiah 40:13; Romans 11:34). On occasion, we've
all tried to counsel God about how to run this world. He
doesn't seem to be very interested in our ideas. How
foolish for us to think that we can counsel Him. "My
thoughts are not your thoughts, neither are your ways
my ways, saith the Lord. For as the heavens are higher
than the earth, so are my ways higher than your ways,
and my thoughts than your thoughts" (Isaiah 55:8-9).

**For he saith to Moses, I will have mercy on whom I
will have mercy, and I will have compassion on whom
I will have compassion** (9:15). God has the right to do
whatever He wishes. If He has mercy or compassion on some
people, no one can fault Him for that. I thank Him for His
mercy and compassion on me.

**So then it is not of him that willeth, nor of him that
runneth, but of God that showeth mercy** (9:16). The
work of God's favor is out of my hands. It isn't found by desire
or effort "of him that willeth." I may have worked hard for

the Lord, but God's favor isn't found "of him that runneth." "To God be the glory, great things He hath done," says the hymn. Salvation is of the Lord.

For the scripture saith unto Pharaoh, Even for this same purpose have I raised thee up, that I might show my power in thee, and that my name might be declared throughout all the earth. Therefore hath he mercy on whom he will have mercy, and whom he will he hardeneth. Thou wilt say then unto me, Why doth he yet find fault? For who hath resisted his will? (9:17-19).

How can God blame me for being what I am, since I'm only what He's made me? If God has chosen to harden my heart, how can He punish me for it? Since He hardened Pharaoh's heart, how could He hold Pharaoh responsible for his evil? Who can resist God's will?

The Book of Exodus tells us that "the Lord hardened the heart of Pharaoh." The Hebrew word for "hardened" means "made firm." God simply confirmed Pharaoh's own decision, but He didn't make the decision for him. If you should harden your heart against God and choose to go to hell, God will make firm your decision. You say, "That's unfair! I want Him to break me down and change my mind." However, it is fair. If you're uncomfortable around God and want nothing to do with Him, why should He force you to live in His presence forever? If you're miserable around Him, God won't save you. He'll let you spend eternity in the abysmal darkness far from heaven. Yet you object, "That's unfair!"

Nay but, O man, who art thou that repliest against God? (9:20a). A good question. Who are you to argue with God?

Shall the thing formed say to him that formed it, Why hast thou made me thus? Hath not the potter power over the clay, of the same lump to make one vessel unto honour,

and another unto dishonour? (9:20b-21). A potter puts the clay on his wheel and cuts it in half. With one half he can make a beautiful vessel to hold roses, and with the other half he can make a spittoon. The potter has the right to make whatever he wants with his clay. Can the clay that was made into a spittoon say, "Why did you make me like this?" The clay has no power over its destiny. It's in the hands of the potter.

The thought of God's sovereignty is frightening. In fact, the doctrine of the sovereignty of God would terrify me if I didn't know the full truth. When I realize that God is love, all fear is suddenly gone. Without this knowledge, I would resist God and His touch . "Will you make me into a garbage pail?" Only when I know that God loves me and chooses the best for me can I yield to the Master Potter.

The potter knows what he wants to make when he begins to work on a lump of clay. The clay only discovers the intent of the potter by yielding to the potter's touch. God has a concept of what He wants me to be when He starts to work in my life. I can only find the mind of God by yielding to His touch.

What if God, willing to show his wrath, and to make his power known, endured with much longsuffering the vessels of wrath fitted to destruction (9:22). God had such patience with Pharaoh! He endured Pharaoh's rebukes and stubbornness to show the world both His patience with the rebellious and His wrath on them.

And that he might make known the riches of his glory on the vessels of mercy, which he had afore prepared unto glory (9:23). Since God can do what He wants, He can make some vessels fit for destruction by His wrath and others fit for glory by His mercy.

God wants to bestow His mercy upon you as a vessel. He prepares, molds, and fits you for the glory He wants you to experience in the presence of His love. The ball is in your court. God offers you His mercy through Jesus Christ, and you can accept it or reject it.

To avoid heresy, these two truths—God's sovereignty and the responsibility of man—need to be kept in balance. In Chapter 10 we'll take a closer look at the second truth, man's responsibility to God's call.

Even us, whom he hath called, not of the Jews only, but also of the Gentiles (9:24). As God promised through the prophets, the Gentiles now equally share His mercy with the Jews.

As he saith also in Hosea, I will call them my people, which were not my people; and her beloved, which was not beloved. And it shall come to pass, that in the place where it was said unto them, Ye are not my people; there shall they be called the children of the living God. Isaiah also crieth concerning Israel, Though the number of the children of Israel be as the sand of the sea, a remnant shall be saved (9:25-27). A Jew has no guarantee of salvation and not all of Israel shall be saved.

For he will finish the work, and cut it short in righteousness: because a short work will the Lord make upon the earth. And as Isaiah said before, Except the Lord of Sabbath had left us a seed, we had been as Sodoma, and been made like unto Gomorrha. What shall we say then? That the Gentiles, which followed not after righteousness, have attained to righteousness, even the righteousness which is of faith. But Israel, which followed after the law of righteousness, hath not attained to the law of righteousness. Wherefore? Because they sought it not by faith, but as it were by the works of the law. For they stumbled at that stumblingstone; as it is writ-

**ten, Behold, I lay in Sion a stumblingstone
and rock of offence: and whosoever believeth on him shall not be ashamed** (9:28-33).

Jesus is the "stumblingstone." The whole idea of righteousness by faith simply confounded the legalistic Jews.
They continued to seek righteousness by the Law, even after
the Cross of Calvary. However, no man has kept the Law
perfectly and attained to righteousness by it. As Peter said
about the Law, "Why... put a yoke upon the neck of the
disciples, which neither our fathers nor we were able to bear?"
(Acts 15 :10). Its fulfillment is beyond the best of men.

In this last section of Chapter 9 Paul says that the Gentiles, who don't even know the Law of Moses, have found the
righteousness of God through faith in Jesus Christ. The Jews,
continuing to seek righteousness through the Law, have never
been able to attain it. How glorious is this righteousness
credited to the sinner who believes in Jesus Christ!

Paul had written to the Philippians about his past advan-
tages as a Jew. "If any other man thinketh that he hath
whereof he might trust in the flesh, I more: circumcised the
eighth day, of the stock of Israel, of the tribe of Benjamin, an
Hebrew of the Hebrews; as touching the law, a Pharisee;
concerning zeal, persecuting the church; touching the righteousness which is in the law, blameless. But what thing
were gain to me, those I counted loss... for the excellency of
the knowledge of Christ Jesus my Lord: for whom I have
suffered the loss of all things, and do count them but refuse,
that I may win Christ, and be found in him, not having mine
own righteousness, which is of the law, but that which is
through the faith of Christ, the righteousness which is of God
by faith" (Philippians 3:4-9).

The Jews of the Old Testament couldn't approach God
When Moses went up to Mount Sinai, they told him, "Go up
and talk to God, then tell us what He said. We're afraid to go
near the place." Seeing the thunder, lightning, and fire roll-

ing around the mountain, the Jews had reason to fear the presence of God. They even cordoned off the mountain and forbade anyone to come near lest he be killed.

The Law that God established with the Jews was one of exclusion, separating them from His presence. An ordinary Jew wouldn't dare enter the Holy Place of the temple; only a true priest had access to it. The common Jew would never dream of entering the Holy of Holies. Only the high priest after many ritual washings and sacrifices could approach it and then only once a year. As a precaution during the high priest's yearly service, the other priests tied a rope around his foot and attached bells to the base of his robe. Should the ringing of the bells ever stop while he was in the Holy of Holies, those outside knew that he had been struck dead. They would then pull him out with the end of the rope.

Under the Law God was inapproachable and man was excluded from His presence. Why? Because a sinful man would be consumed in the presence of a righteous God. Only one thing today prevents a man from dying in God's presence— Jesus Christ.

God has accounted me as righteous, and I have access to Him at any time. I have attained the righteousness of the Law through my faith in Jesus Christ. The Jews under the Law are excluded, for they in futility try to find righteousness through the works of the Law. "As it is written, Behold, I lay in Sion a stumblingstone and rock of offence: and whosoever believeth on him shall not be ashamed" (Romans 9:33; cf. Isaiah 28: 16).

The Jews have stumbled over the stumbling stone for two millenniums. "But we preach Christ crucified," Paul said, "unto the Jews a stumblingblock, and unto the Greeks foolishness; but unto them which are called, both Jews and Greeks, Christ the power of God" to salvation (I Corinthians 1:23-24).

CHAPTER 10
SAVED

Brethren, my heart's desire and prayer to God for Israel is, that they might be saved (10:1). "I'm not bitter against the Jews," Paul is saying. "My heart's desire and prayer for these people is for their salvation.

"For I bear them record that they have a zeal of God, but not according to knowledge (10:2). Even today the orthodox Jews have an extreme zeal toward God. When some young Israelis near Rosh Pina recently accepted Jesus Christ as their Messiah, several orthodox Jews broke into their home, beat them up, and damaged their house. Such zeal for God certainly isn't according to knowledge.

For they being ignorant of God's righteousness, and going about to establish their own righteousness, have not submitted themselves unto the righteousness of God (10:3). God has established a righteousness for all men through faith in Jesus Christ. Without Him, men seek righteousness by their own rules and standards. "I think that this is the right thing to do in this situation. I believe that is the wrong thing to do." However, the guidelines of men don't meet God's requirements.

All men have standards they live by, even those men who teach situational ethics. Let's say that a professor stands before a class. He claims that there are no absolutes—all standards depend upon the mores of society, truth must be experienced by the individual, and right and wrong must be personally interpreted. Should a student get up in the middle of the lecture, walk to the front, sit at the professor's desk, and start rummaging through his papers, the professor would shout, "Stop that! You're out of order!"

"Do you mean that I'm doing something wrong?" the student could ask. "Who says it's wrong? There's no absolute basis of right and wrong. Every man has to experience truth for himself." In reality, all men have certain basic concepts that define actions as right or wrong, even though some deny this fact. Men live by the standards they have set, but their standards, no matter how high, are unacceptable to God.

The Bible says that our righteous acts are as filthy rags in the sight of God (Isaiah 64:6). I can parade my good deeds before God. "Look at me! How do you like this new suit?" Filthy rags! Paul said that he wanted to "be found in him, not having mine own righteousness, which is of the law, but that which is through the faith of Christ, the righteousness which is of God by faith" (Philippians 3:9).

For Christ is the end of the law for righteousness to every one that believeth (10:4). Laws or rules cannot make me righteous. Only one thing can do so: my faith in Jesus Christ. God imparts His righteousness to me by my faith. If anyone thinks he can improve on that, good luck!

For Moses describeth the righteousness which is of the law, That the man which doeth those things shall live by them (10:5). The righteousness of the Law was based on what man must do. The righteousness of faith is based on what Jesus Christ has done. The finished work of Christ forms the basis of my righteous standing before God. His work is completed, whereas my righteousness by the Law is continually in progress.

You may obey the Law for 85 years and then make one mistake. What a shame! The Bible says, "Cursed be he that confirmeth [upholds] not all the words of this law to do them" (Deuteronomy 27:26a). "For whosoever shall keep the whole law, and yet offend in one point, he is guilty of all" (James 2:10). If you're seeking righteousness by the Law, you're in a dangerous place. If you're seeking righteousness by Jesus Christ, you're in the only safe place. God has finished the work for you.

But the righteousness which is of faith speaketh on this wise, Say not in thine heart, Who shall ascend into heaven? (that is, to bring Christ down from above:) or, Who shall descend into the deep? (that is, to bring up Christ again from the dead.) But what saith it? The word is nigh thee, even in thy mouth, and in thy heart: that is, the word of faith, which we preach; that if thou shalt confess with thy mouth the Lord Jesus, and shalt believe in thine heart that God hath raised him from the dead, thou shalt be saved (10:6-9).

How close are you to true righteousness? "Oh, it's so difficult! I must practically ascend into heaven, perform glorious deeds, and bring Christ down from above. I must descend into the deep and raise Him again from the dead." No such rigid requirements have been given, for true righteousness is as near to you as your mouth. **If thou shalt confess with thy mouth that Jesus Christ is Lord, and shalt believe in thine heart that God hath raised him from the dead, thou shalt be saved. For with the heart man believeth unto righteousness; and with the mouth confession is made unto salvation** (10:9-10). With the confession of your mouth God regards your past sinful deeds as non-existent. When you're that close to salvation, it's folly to be lost. Confess with your mouth that Jesus Christ is the Lord, believe in your heart that God raised Him from the dead, and you'll be saved.

For whosoever shall call upon the name of the Lord shall be saved (10:13). We discussed the sovereignty of God in the last chapter. Now we come to the matter of human responsibility. Here the truth finds balance. If you confess Him and believe in Him, He'll save you, because He keeps His word. "But what if I'm not predestined?" You'll be saved anyhow. No one who has called upon the name of the Lord has been turned away. "God be merciful to me a sinner" (Luke 18:13b) is a prayer that has always been answered, for God delights to show mercy. So, you're responsible for calling upon the name of the Lord. And when you do, you'll be saved.

For the scripture saith, Whosoever believeth on him shall not be ashamed. For there is no difference between the Jew and the Greek: for the same Lord over all is rich unto all that call upon him (10:11-12). God is no less eager to save a Gentile than to save a Jew. Sometimes we show a preference toward the Jews, because we're so anxious to have their spiritual eyes opened again. But God isn't placing any special emphasis upon them today. **For whosoever shall call upon the name of the Lord shall be saved** (10:13). All men are equal in His eyes. However, God will deal again with Israel, as we'll see in the next chapter.

How then shall they call on him in whom they have not believed? How can people call upon Him unless they have believed in Him? **And how shall they believe in him of whom they have not heard? and how shall they hear without a preacher? and how shall they preach, except they be sent?** (10:14-15a). Here Paul follows a chain of thought. Why would men call upon someone in whom they don't believe? How can they believe in Him unless they hear about Him? How can they hear about Him unless a preacher has been sent?

The whole missionary thrust of the Church is expressed in these verses. We send out missionaries for people to hear, believe, and be saved. **As it is written, How beautiful are the feet of them that preach the gospel of peace, and bring glad tidings of good things** (10:15b). All Christians share the good things of the Gospel of Christ with a hopeless world.

But they have not all obeyed the gospel. For Isaiah saith, Lord, who hath believed our report? So then faith cometh by hearing, and hearing by the word of God (10:16-17). The term in verse 17 translated as "word" isn't logos, which often refers to Christ the living Word, but rhema, the spoken word of God.

But I say, Have they not heard? Yes verily, their sound went into all the earth, and their words unto the ends of the world (10:18). Paul is quoting from the Psalms. "The heavens declare the glory of God; and the firmament showeth his handiwork. Day unto day uttereth speech, and night unto night showeth knowledge. There is no speech nor language, where their voice is not heard" (Psalm 19:1-3). What does this passage mean? Nature testifies to man about the existence of God. "Have they not heard?" (10:18). Yes, they surely have heard!

But I say, Did not Israel know? First Moses saith, I will provoke you to jealousy by them that are no people, and by a foolish nation I will anger you. But Isaiah is very bold, and saith, I was found of them that sought me not; I was made manifest unto them that asked not after me. But to Israel he saith, All day long I have stretched forth my hands unto a disobedient and gainsaying [obstinate] people (10:19-21). Paul tosses back to the Jews their own Scriptures. Even Moses, their father and greatest leader, prophesied that God would stretch out His hand to the Gentiles (Deuteronomy 32:21). God did this to provoke the Jews to jealousy, as they see His grace and goodness bestowed upon Gentiles, the outcasts.

Rather than condemn the Jews for their legalistic attitude toward God, we should demonstrate His love in our midst, the power of the Spirit, and the joy of our Redeemer and Messiah. In our efforts to evangelize the Jews, we should show such a love and excitement about the Messiah that the Jews are provoked to jealousy. Let them stop and say, "He's our Messiah, you know!" And well they should, for He is.

CHAPTER 11
NATURAL AND SPIRITUAL ISRAEL

I say then, Hath God cast away his people? (11:1a). This is an important question. Some preachers today are saying, "God has cast away His people." They claim that all the prophecies concerning the natural branch of Israel were fulfilled when Titus destroyed the nation in A.D. 70. They believe that God is now through with the Jews.

I receive many letters from people who read my books and try to correct me for what they think is my misunderstanding of prophecy. They believe that the Israel of the Old Testament is the Church of today and the Jews of the Bible are now the Christians. In their minds all the present and future prophecies for Israel and the Jews find fulfillment in the Church. Such an interpretation leads these people to an incorrect view of biblical prophecy. Almost without exception, everyone who teaches that the Jews have had their chance and God has cut them off also teaches that the Church will go through the Great Tribulation.

But God hasn't cut off His people. **Hath God cast away his people? God forbid [perish the thought]. For I also am an Israelite, of the seed of Abraham, of the tribe of Benjamin. God hath not cast away his people which he foreknew** (11:1-2a).

Wot [know] ye not what the scripture saith of Elijah? how he maketh intercession to God against

Israel (11:2b). Notice that Elijah made intercession against Israel, not for her. How would you feel if a pastor prayed against you? Elijah prayed, **Lord, they [Israelites] have killed thy prophets, and digged down thine altars; and I am left alone, and they seek my life** (11:3). Elijah thought things couldn't get worse. "They've killed everybody who loves You. I'm the only one left, and they're trying to kill me. You're almost out of troops, Lord!"

How did God answer the distraught prophet? **I have reserved to myself seven thousand men, who have not bowed the knee to the image of Baal. Even so then at this present time also there is a remnant according to the election of grace** (11:4-5). That "present time" holds to our day. God has a remnant among the Jews who believe and trust in Jesus as their Messiah. They share in the glorious blessings of God just as we Christians do.

And if by grace, then is it no more of works: otherwise grace is no more grace. But if it be of works, then is it no more grace: otherwise work is no more work (11:6). I'm accepted by God either wholly by my works or wholly by His grace. I can't be accepted partly by one and partly by the other. If I'm accepted by grace then works have nothing to do with my salvation. The Good News is that my acceptance is wholly by His grace.

What then? Israel hath not obtained that which he seeketh for; but the election hath obtained it, and the rest were blinded (according as it is written, God hath given them the spirit of slumber, eyes that they should not see, and ears that they should not hear;) unto this day (11:7-8). Israel has been blinded by God. Those Jews still trying to relate to God through the Law haven't yet received His grace.

In fact, the Jews don't even keep the covenant of the Law anymore. You say, "They observe the Sabbath, light their candles, eat their kosher meals, have their washings, and such." Yes, but where are the sacrifices for their sins? They have none. They seek to approach God totally through works. Their religion is the same as Cain's, presenting the works of their hands. As God rejected Cain, so He's rejecting the Jews and the works offered in atonement for their sins. Good works never cover a man's sins. The Jews have been blinded, because they have rejected the grace offered by God through Jesus the Messiah.

And David saith, Let their table be made a snare, and a trap, and a stumblingblock, and a recompense unto them: let their eyes be darkened, that they may not see, and bow down their back always (11:9-10). Paul quotes from one of the messianic psalms prophesying the death of Jesus Christ. "In my thirst they gave me vinegar to drink" (Psalm 69:21b). This psalm prophesies the words of Christ, and these words have been fulfilled upon Israel. The "table" of communion by which the Jews once came to God has become a stumbling block, because they reject the significance of Christ's Last Supper. Their backs are bowed down and their eyes are darkened to His truth.

I say then, Have they stumbled that they should fall? God forbid: but rather through their fall salvation is come unto the Gentiles, for to provoke them to jealousy (11:11). Are the Jews entirely removed from God's plan? No. They've been broken off temporarily from the good olive tree, but they'll be grafted in again. While the Jews are temporarily cut off, the door has been opened for the Gentiles to enter into God's grace.

Now if the fall of them be the riches of the world, and the diminishing of them the riches of the Gentiles; how much more their fulness? (11:12). If bless-

ings have come to us through their fall, how much greater
the blessings when the Jews enter their fullness. What
will this blessing be? The Kingdom Age.

God will restore the Jews to His love and favor when
He opens their eyes and they receive Christ. The fullness of the glorious kingdom of God will then be come.
Zechariah testified to this day, saying, "And one shall
say unto him, What are these wounds in thine hands?
Then he shall answer, Those with which I was wounded
in the house of my friends" (Zechariah 13:6). Again the
prophet said, "And they shall look upon me whom they
have pierced, and they shall mourn for him, as one
mourneth for his only son, and shall be in bitterness
for him, as one that is in bitterness for his firstborn"
(Zechariah 12:10b). One day the Jews will realize their
blindness and folly. They'll accept Jesus Christ, and
the glorious national restoration of these people will
bring in the Kingdom Age.

**For I speak to you Gentiles, inasmuch as I am
the apostle of the Gentiles, I magnify mine office: if
by any means I may provoke to emulation [jeal-
ousy] them which are my flesh, and might save
some of them** (11:13-14). Paul certainly did arouse their
emotions. The Jews considered his ministry to the Gentiles as sacrilegious.

Just his presence in the temple once provoked the Jews
to try to kill Paul. When order had been restored by the
soldiers, Paul began talking to the Jews in their tongue.
"Brothers, listen to me! I've lived all my life as a good
Jew. I was zealous just like you. I understand your feelings. I tried to stop this new heresy. I persecuted these
Christians. The high priest and all the Council can tes-
tify of my zeal.

"In fact, I was on my way to Damascus to persecute
the Church there. About noon as I neared the city, a light

came from heaven. I fell on the ground and heard a voice saying, 'Why do you persecute me?' I said, 'Who are you, Lord? I want to serve you.' The voice answered, 'I am Jesus whom you are persecuting. I am going to send you to the Gentiles."

When the Jews heard this, they began to scream, taking their coats off and throwing dirt in the air. "Kill him! Rid the earth of him ! He doesn't deserve to live !" (Acts 21:27-22:23). Why? Because Paul claimed that God had sent him to the Gentiles with the message of salvation. Such a claim provoked the Jews to frenzy.

For if the casting away of them be the reconciling of the world—if God was able to reconcile the Gentile world to Himself by their rejection—**what shall the receiving of them be, but life from the dead?** (11:15). God's future acceptance of the Jews will bring life, the Kingdom Age, to the world.

For if the firstfruit be holy, the lump is also holy: and if the root be holy, so are the branches. And if some of the branches [Jews] be broken off, and thou, being a wild olive tree [Gentiles], were grafted in among them, and with them partakest of the root and fatness of the olive tree (11:16-17). As a Gentile, a wild branch, I've been grafted into the tree of the promises, covenants, and blessings of God. By being grafted into Christ, I'm a partaker of God's promises and a beneficiary of all the promises to Israel.

Boast not against the branches. But if thou boast, thou bearest not the root, but the root thee (11:18). You're not holding yourself up, the root is supporting you. So don't boast. You stand only by the grace of God and the mercies of Jesus Christ.

Thou wilt say, then, The branches were broken off, that I might be grafted in. Well; because of unbelief they were broken off, and thou standest by

faith. Be not highminded, but fear (11:19-20). We must not boast against the Jews or look down on them. We should never think, "God cut them off so that I might be grafted in." We've been grafted in by faith—not because we're worthy, or deserving, or because God saw something special in us. We stand by faith. They were cut off because of unbelief.

For if God spared not the natural branches, take heed lest He also spare not thee (11:21). Since God cut off the natural branches, then the wild branch that's been grafted in can also be cut off.

Behold therefore the goodness and severity of God: on them which fell, severity; but toward thee, goodness, if thou continue in his goodness: otherwise thou also shalt be cut off (11:22). Your standing with God therefore appears to be conditional; you must continue in His goodness. Jesus said, "Abide in me, and I in you. As the branch cannot bear fruit of itself, except it abide in the vine; no more can ye, except ye abide in me... If a man abide not in me, he is cast forth as a branch, and is withered; and men gather them, and cast them into the fire, and they are burned" (John 15:4,6).

And they also, if they abide not still in unbelief—if the Jews cease in their unbelief of Christ—**shall be grafted in: for God is able to graft them in again. For if thou wert cut out of the olive tree which is wild by nature, and wert grafted contrary to nature into a good olive tree: how much more shall these, which be the natural branches, be grafted into their own olive tree? For I would not, brethren, that ye should be ignorant of this mystery, lest ye should be wise in your own conceits; that blindness in part is happened to Israel, until the fulness of the Gentiles be come in** (11:23-25).

This blindness has happened to Israel until "the fulness of the Gentiles be come in." This indicates that God has chosen a certain number among the Gentiles to believe. They constitute the fullness of the Gentiles. I believe that the moment the last Gentile chosen by God surrenders his life to Jesus Christ and is born again that this dispensation will come to an immediate close. The Lord will then gather His Church to Himself, and God will once again deal with the nation Israel as His people.

In Daniel 9 the angel told Daniel that there were seventy sevens determined upon the nation Israel. From the time that the commandment goes forth to restore and rebuild Jerusalem to the coming of the Messiah the Prince would be 69 sevens. The angel then said that the Messiah would be cut off without receiving for Himself (the kingdom). The seventieth seven-year cycle of Daniel is yet future. Jesus referred to it in Matthew 24 as the time when the Antichrist will stand in the Holy Place. In II Thessalonians 2:4 Paul said that this Antichrist will there declare that he is God. This has not yet happened, so it's yet to come. Thus, we're still in the time of the Gentiles, waiting for the fullness of the Gentiles to come in.

And so all Israel shall be saved: as it is written, There shall come out of Sion the Deliverer, and shall turn away ungodliness from Jacob: for this is my covenant unto them, when I shall take away their sins. As concerning the gospel, they are enemies for your sakes: but as touching the election, they are beloved for the fathers' sakes. For the gifts and calling of God are without repentance (11:26-29). God hasn't changed. He has called the Jews, and they're still His elect.

Notice that God calls these future Jewish believers His "election." This helps us to understand the proph-

ecy in Matthew's gospel. "Immediately after the tribulation of those days... they shall see the Son of man
coming in the clouds of heaven with power and great
glory. And he shall send his angels with a great sound
of a trumpet, and they shall gather together his elect
from the four winds, from one end of heaven to the
other" (Matthew 24:29-31). The "elect" refers to Jewish
believers, and these prophecies in Matthew 24 are on
Jewish ground.

Some Christians use Matthew 24 as proof that the
Church won't be gathered to Christ until after the Tribulation and the return of Jesus. Not so. This passage will
be the fulfillment of God's promise to His elect people,
the Jews.

Jesus said, "Pray ye that your flight be not in the
winter, neither on the Sabbath day" (Matthew 24:20).
How many Christians would hesitate to travel on a Saturday, the Sabbath? We're free to travel as much as we
want in all directions on Saturday. However, a Jew seeking righteousness by the Law cannot walk more than
two-thirds of a mile on the Sabbath day.

Some people say that God has cut off Israel and is
finished with them. No, "God forbid." As Augustine said,
"If you understand the dispensations, everything else is
simple." Thinking that God is finished with Israel brings
confusion. The greatest revival in the world is yet to take
place, as God again draws these people to Himself, opens
their eyes, and they recognize Him. What a beautiful day
that will be!

**For as ye in times past have not believed God,
yet have now obtained mercy through their unbelief: even so have these also now not believed, that
through your mercy they also may obtain mercy.
For God hath concluded them all in unbelief, that
he might have mercy upon all** (11:30-32). The mercy

of God has now been extended to all men. The Jews are now in unbelief. In this position they're able to receive the mercy of God.

O the depth of the riches both of the wisdom and knowledge of God! how unsearchable are his judgments, and his ways past finding out! (11:33). We've been looking at the ways of God—His sovereignty, calling, election—and we find these difficult to understand. For years I sought to reconcile divine sovereignty and human responsibility, eternal security and free moral agency. I pondered them, but I found it futile to search the judgments of God.

One day in exasperation I slammed down my fist and said, "God, I cannot reconcile Your sovereignty with my responsibility!" God spoke to my heart clearly and said, "I never asked you to reconcile it. I only asked you to believe it." I've had peace ever since.

I still cannot reconcile the difficulties, but I don't have to. I just accept and believe in these truths which remain to me irreconcilable. God is absolutely sovereign and can do whatever He wants. He can harden my heart, show me mercy, damn me, or save me. I believe that I can choose to call upon the Lord and be saved. He is sovereign, yet I have the choice. Though I cannot reconcile that, I believe it.

For who hath known the mind of the Lord? (11:34a). How can I understand the mind of God or think as He thinks? "Such knowledge is too wonderful for me; it is high, I cannot attain unto it" (Psalm 139:6). **Or who hath been his counsellor?** (11:34b). God doesn't need my advice. He can run the universe without me telling Him how to do it. How many times have I been so foolish as to try to counsel God?

Or who hath first given to him, and it shall be recompensed unto him again? (11:35). God will not be a debtor to any man. Jesus said, "Give, and it shall be given unto you; good measure, pressed down, and shaken together, and running over" (Luke 6:38). This is one of the spiritual laws that God has established in the world. We're familiar with the natural laws of the universe, such as electricity, magnetism, and gravity, and we've learned to use them for our advantage. Though I don't understand how the law of electricity functions, it doesn't keep me from turning on the lights.

People often fail to realize that God has also established spiritual laws as predictable in cause and effect as natural laws. We cannot give to God without Him multiplying back to us. Because we cannot understand how the spiritual laws operate, we often fail to use them. I cannot understand why the more I give to God the more I'll receive, but I know that it works.

For of Him, and through Him, and to Him, are all things: to whom be glory for ever. Amen (11:36). Paul ends Chapter 11 with this wonderful doxology. To God be glory forever! For it's all wrapped up in Him. The universe with all its processes, all the realms of understanding and logic, all the love, mercy, and grace belong to Him.

CHAPTER 12
THE LIVING SACRIFICE

In several of his Epistles Paul gently but earnestly uses the phrase, "I beseech you." This is the way God talks to us. He doesn't say, "I demand this!" Rather, He speaks to us quite tenderly. **I beseech you therefore, brethren** (12:1a).

"Therefore" always refers to a prior thought and links the present statement with it. This "therefore" takes us back to the comments on the love, mercy, and grace of God which have provided our election, calling, justification, and glorification. Because we're now justified, Paul urges, **by the mercies of God, that ye present your bodies a living sacrifice, holy, acceptable unto God, which is your reasonable service** (12:1b).

"Reasonable" is translated from a Greek word meaning "logical." To commit my life to God for His direction is logical, because God knows the end of a matter from the beginning. God's wisdom is so much greater than mine. He has never made a mistake and never will. I have made many mistakes and still do. It makes good sense to seek His counsel and guidance and to give my life over to His direction.

God could work apart from human instruments. He could use angels to do His work, and they could probably do a much better job. I wish He would use His angels instead of some of the hucksters I've seen on television.

In any event, God has chosen to use people like you and me to do His work.

Rather than offer a slain sacrifice as in the Old Testament, you're to offer your body as a living sacrifice. Present your body as an instrument in God's hands, and He'll use you to accomplish His work in the hearts and lives of those around you.

And be not conformed to this world (12:2a). Immense pressures are working to conform you to this world's system. If you don't conform, the advertising agencies make you think that you're missing out on life. Peer pressure and the mores of society are powerful instruments in Satan's hands. Yet we're told, **Be ye transformed by the renewing of your mind** (12:2b).

A great difference exists between "conformed" and "transformed." Earlier in Romans Paul said, "Ye are not in the flesh, but in the Spirit, if so be that the Spirit of God dwell in you. Now if any man have not the Spirit of Christ, he is none of his" (Romans 8:9). Paul was explaining the two sides of man's nature, flesh and spirit. Being "Transformed by the renewing of your mind" means that your mind is no longer occupied with the fleshly side of your nature.

Many people seek to relate man to animals, because they want to live like them. Animals don't possess a spirit and live solely on a body-conscious level. So, the man who wants to feel free of any responsibility to God disclaims his spiritual capacities and proclaims himself a highly evolved animal. He's constantly searching for the missing link between himself and the ape. Natural man does have a missing link, but it's not between man and the animal kingdom, but between man and God. Man, once created in the image of God, has fallen from the spirit-controlled being he once was to the flesh-controlled creature he has become. Now God seeks to restore man into His image by the new birth.

Jesus said, "That which is born of the flesh is flesh; and that which is born of the Spirit is spirit. Marvel not that I said unto thee, Ye must be born again" (John 3:6-7). The mind of the flesh is death, but the mind of the Spirit is life and peace (Romans 8:6). By living on the spiritual side of life, your mind is occupied with the things of God. By this transformation from flesh to spirit, you're born again and your mind is renewed.

That ye may prove what is that good, and acceptable, and perfect, will of God (12:2c). The desire expressed in many hearts is: "If I only knew God's will for my life." So many want to do the perfect will of God, but unfortunately don't know what it is.

Here Paul gives a two-step method for knowing the will of God for your life. First, present your body to God. Writing to the Corinthians, Paul asked, "Don't you know that your body is the temple of the Holy Spirit?" (I Corinthians 6:19). God has made a claim on your body, and He wants you to yield it to Him so that it's under the control of His Spirit. Second, you must not be conformed to this dead world, but be transformed in your mind to the world of the Spirit. When you present your body as an instrument in God's hand, you become a non-conformist to this world of sin and you're transformed by His Spirit. Then you find God's will for your life.

I believe that God reveals His will to me daily. I get up in the morning and say, "God, today my life is Yours. My body is available for You to use as You see fit. Lead me, guide me, and work out Your perfect will in my life." God reveals His will to me, because I've asked Him and trust Him to do just that.

Too often we assume that God only reveals His will in exotic ways such as tinglings down the spine or fiery letters in the sky. When I entered Bible college, I learned that some students had seen visions or messages emblazoned in the sky calling them into the ministry. I didn't have any such experiences. Actually, I had the least spectacular call to the ministry of anyone in school. All I had was a desire to serve God by learning more of His Word.

After all these years I'm one of the few from my class still in the ministry. Many former classmates are selling cars or working in some such occupation. I sometimes wonder what happened to those fiery letters in the sky.

When we expect the will or call of God to come in dramatic ways, we don't anticipate the natural ways by which He so often leads us. Many times during the day God's hand is leading me, but I'm not even aware of it.

Some people expect a divine signal system to give them directions. "Turn left! Beep! Beep! Go forward..." They're looking for the spectacular, so they bemoan the fact that they've never been led by God. In looking over my life's situations, I realize that God has worked out things with perfect timing. My hindsight shows me that my promptings to do a particular thing had come from God.

God leads us in natural ways. He said that He would write His Law on the tablets of our hearts (II Corinthians 3:3). He places in our hearts the desire to do a particular thing. After we do it, we realize that the prompting came from God. It's wonderful to realize that we were listening to God, got His message straight, and played a part in a particular circumstance for His glory. The awareness of God's hand upon our lives is an overwhelming and humbling experience.

So often God leads us one step at a time. In the midst of a successful revival in Samaria, Philip was told by God, "Go down to Gaza, which is desert." Philip obeyed the prompting of God, and when he came to Gaza he saw the chariot with the Ethiopian eunuch. The Lord said, "Go near and join him" (Acts 8:26-29). The second step in the leading didn't come until Philip had obeyed the first. If he had disobeyed the first command, he never would have received the second. Thus, he never would have known what God's will was for him in Gaza. We often demand to know God's reasoning; but the revelation of His will to our lives is progressive, as we obey step by step.

For I say, through the grace given unto me, to every man that is among you, not to think of himself more highly than he ought to think; but to think soberly, according as God hath dealt to every man the measure of faith (12:3). Thinking more highly of myself than I ought is one of my greatest problems in serving God. In trying to find the reasons why God chose me, I sometimes think that He knew He could trust me. However, God uses me simply because He wants to. As a human instrument, I must beware the danger of accepting the glory that belongs to God. Lest I ever be puffed up because God uses me, I remember the instrument that He chose to speak to Balaam: a simple donkey (Numbers 22:22-33).

When God places the anointing of His Spirit on you as His instrument, people will oftentimes magnify you as someone special. You can't stop them, but you can refuse to accept their plaudits. When Peter and John were used by God to heal the lame man in the temple, the people gathered around Peter. They looked at him in awe, as if to say, "You must be a very holy man for God to use you."

Peter pointed to the healed man and said, "Men of Israel, why do you marvel at this? Why do you stare at us as though we through our own power or godliness have made this fellow walk? This is the power of Jesus Christ demonstrated to you. Glorify Him!" (Acts 3:1-16).

Peter knew that he was a blunderer and a weakling. Jesus had told him, "The spirit indeed is willing, but the flesh is weak" (Matthew 26:41b). So when the Lord anointed and used him, Peter wasn't about to take any credit for it.

When God begins to anoint you, don't take the credit. Paul asked, "What do you have that you did not receive?" (I Corinthians 4:7b). If you've been given a talent, ability, or gift, why go around as though it came from you? If God didn't put intelligence in you, you'd be a babbling idiot. You can think and reason only because He has given you the ability. So never magnify yourself or your abilities.

Because of the beautiful inspiration of the Spirit, I'll occasionally deliver a really good sermon. Once, after an especially good one, I was walking toward the back of the church and the devil was on my shoulder. He said, "You gave a great sermon! You really blessed the people today!"

The Lord was speaking to me also. He said, "What did you give but what you received?" I said, "Nothing, Lord." He said, "Then you won't take credit for it, will you?" I said, "No way, Lord!" Whatever I have has come from God. Paul says that every man ought **to think soberly, according as God hath dealt to every man the measure of faith** (12:3b). Man has a tendency to exalt the idea of faith, and this can easily become a matter of spiritual pride. "God does such wonderful things through me because of my great faith." As though a man's faith was at the center of God's great work!

Paul said, "By grace are ye saved through faith; and that not of yourselves: it is the gift of God" (Ephesians 2:8). You may say, "What? We don't get any credit?" No. God gave us the necessary measure of faith to believe in the grace that He was offering. If He hadn't given us that faith, we couldn't believe. We'd still be out in the dark, looking in.

Peter explained to the wondering throng how the lame man was walking and leaping: "Yes, the faith which is by Him..." (Acts 3:16). The faith for the miracle had come by Jesus Christ. Peter wasn't even claiming the faith as his own. This is quite revealing in light of all the proddings we receive nowadays to greater faith. Faith is God's gift to us, and He has given to each man a measure of faith.

For as we have many members in one body, and all members have not the same office: so we, being many, are one body in Christ, and every one members one of another (12:4-5). After going to such great lengths to bring Christians together, God must grieve over a body that is so divided, splintered, and antagonistic. Be thankful that your body isn't in the same shape as the Church body, where one eye wants nothing to do with the other because it doesn't see things exactly the same way. At times the body of Christ must look spastic with its fightings, jealousies, and divisions. How tragic to see members tearing one another down.

What does a non-Christian think when he sees the division in the body of Christ? He goes away with the impression that the body of Christ is sick.

Though it is one, the body has many members, and every part has a different purpose. We're members one of another. In a sense, the Holy Spirit is the nervous system coordinating the work of the body. Under His direction the parts work together smoothly to make a strong witness to the world. I thank God for the body's witness when the Spirit is directing it. As Paul wrote to the Romans, "Your faith is spoken of throughout the whole world" (Romans 1:8b). Our faith is known worldwide when the body is functioning properly. If only we'd forget our denominational allegiances!

I don't think that all Christians should meet in the same church. The variety of gatherings with the different modes of worship is important, as it meets the many particular needs within the body of Christ. However, we shouldn't develop our own exclusive club where we look down on others and say, "They don't worship or teach like we do." Remember, we're one body, and God uses each fellowship as a light to reach the world around it.

Everyone has a function within the body. The ear is as important as the mouth. God has called me to be a mouth, but if you don't have ears to hear, what good is a mouth? The body must have input as well as output.

Having then gifts differing according to the grace that is given to us (12:6a). God gives each one a gift suitable for his ministry within the body. We often ask for gifts, as the Scripture says, "Covet earnestly the best gifts" (I Corinthians 12:31a). For a long time I desired certain gifts that I didn't have. I fasted, prayed, and promised to use them in the right way, but God hasn't seen fit to give them to me. The last time I talked to Him about it, He let me know what my gift was and told me to be satisfied with that.

"But Lord, I want the gift of healing. Think of what I could do with it!"

He said, "Charles, I called you to teach."

God impressed His answer upon my heart, and He told me that He had already bestowed upon me the more excellent way. I said, "Thank You, Lord. I'll take it." It's so exciting to be an instrument through which God shows His love!

If you have the gift of prophecy, then you should **prophesy according to the proportion of faith** (12:6b). What does that mean? Sometimes the Lord will give you an unusual prophecy and you may not have enough faith to speak it. "Lord, is this really from You? What if I speak it and it doesn't happen?" I've been in that boat many times. The Lord has given me prophecies on numerous occasions, but I didn't utter them due to a lack of faith. Once the unspoken prophecy had come true, I wished I had uttered it.

The gift of prophecy must be exercised according to your proportion of faith. Of course, you're putting your gift on the line by speaking. If you utter something in the name of the Lord and it doesn't come to pass, then you— not the Lord —made a mistake.

Or ministry, let us wait on our ministering (12:7a). We often make a mistake by thinking that the ministry means standing behind the pulpit. No, that isn't where real ministry takes place. True ministry means serving one another. Some people have a wonderful way of exercising this gift. Others exercise it so you feel obligated to them, because they keep reminding you of their service. Actually, all the gifts can be exercised in good or bad ways. We need the guidance of the Spirit in using His gifts.

Or he that teacheth, on teaching (12:7b). If your gift is teaching, I believe that you should be first and foremost a student. The Bible says that the Holy Spirit will bring to your remembrance "whatsoever I have said unto you" (John 14:26b). This means that you must have learned His sayings. Thus, the gift of teaching requires diligent study of the Word of God.

Or he that exhorteth, on exhortation (12:8a). Exhortation is an extremely important gift in the Church. Sometimes we need to be pushed in the right direction, like the little boy on the diving board. He wants to jump. Everybody is yelling "Jump!" But he's too scared. He walks off the board, then back on again. He needs someone to come up and give him a push.

The exhorter gives us a little shove in the right direction. He encourages us to trust the Lord, believe the promises of God, and open our hearts in worship and praise to Him. He exhorts us to action by applying the truths of God in our particular walk.

He that giveth, let him do it with simplicity (12:8b). Did you know that there is a gift of giving? Some Christians have this special touch from God. If that is your gift, "do it with simplicity." Otherwise, you can make your giving a complicated matter by wrapping strings around it.

There is also the gift of ruling. **He that ruleth, with diligence** (12:8c). A person with this gift should diligently govern those under his authority.

He that sheweth mercy, with cheerfulness (12:8d). What a valuable gift! When I'm going through a bad time, I don't want to talk with someone who won't sympathize. I need understanding and comfort, so I look for a Christian with the gift of mercy. If you have this gift, exercise it with cheerfulness. Enter into the person's suffering and then lift him with the cheerfulness of the Spirit.

Let love be without dissimulation [be sincere]. Abhor that which is evil (12:9). One of the major weaknesses of the Church is a great tolerance for evil. We've practically established peaceful coexistence with the works of darkness. However, we're supposed to resist them. We need to hate evil and **cleave to that which is good** (12:9b).

Be kindly affectioned one to another with brotherly love; in honour preferring one another (12:10). Each verse in Chapter 12 is a complete message in itself and displays Paul's gift of exhortation in operation.

Not slothful in business; fervent in spirit; serving the Lord (12:11). Christians must consciously do all things as unto the Lord. It hurts me when a Christian separates his business from his spiritual life. Once I did business with a fellow in the church. When I questioned him about the product, he gave me a line that I'd expect to hear from a con man. I also grieve whenever one of the sheep is cheated by another member of the church. The whole concept behind a business operated by a Christian is to serve the Lord. Whatever he does in word or deed should be for God (Colossians 3:17). You can't cheat a brother for the glory of God. Anyone guilty of this is deceived by his own greed. Many divisions sprout up within the body because of these unethical business practices.

Rejoicing in hope (12:12a). It's impossible to rejoice in all circumstances. However, I can always rejoice in the Lord, lifting myself above circumstances and fixing my eyes on Him. I can always rejoice in hope, because I can always hope that the circumstances will improve. "I can't get any lower, but the Lord will see me through!"

the word of God never tells us to rejoice in circumstances themselves. Some people encourage us to do that, but it's unrealistic. I like practical Christianity, and that's what the Bible gives us.

Be **patient in tribulation** (12:12b). "Tribulation worketh patience" (Romans 5:3). As we said before, these two are often tied together. When we pray for patience, we usually experience tribulation. This teaches us the very patience we need.

Continuing instant in prayer; distributing to the necessity of saints; given to hospitality. Bless them which persecute you: bless, and curse not. Rejoice with them that do rejoice, and weep with them that weep. Be of the same mind one toward another. Mind not high things, but condescend to men

of low estate. Be not wise in your own conceits. Recompense to no man evil for evil. Provide things honest in the sight of all men (12:12b-17). This is Paul's exhortation to practical Christianity.

If it be possible, as much as lieth in you, live peaceably with all men (12:18). I'm glad that Paul admits that this is sometimes impossible. Still, we must never be the cause for strife with others. Living peaceably with all men means that we overlook things, ignore statements, and pass off irritations. Sometimes it's much better to pretend that we didn't hear a certain remark. Unfortunately, some people spill out their poison louder a second time. Then we know that peace is impossible. In any case, we're never to curse or lash back at them. Certain people are crude, but that's no excuse for us to act the same way. If they want to have their say, let them. Don't recompense evil for evil.

Paul continues, **Dearly beloved, avenge not yourselves, but rather give place unto wrath: for it is written, Vengeance is mine; I will repay, saith the Lord. Therefore if thine enemy hunger, feed him; if he thirst, give him drink: for in so doing thou shalt heap coals of fire on his head** (12:19-20).

A Scripture may seem obscure because we're not familiar with the customs of the day. Heaping coals of fire on a person's head wasn't a cruel act. In biblical times people carried containers of charcoal on their heads. Sometimes they'd have to walk far to get live coals to start their fire at home. Heaping live coals on someone's head wasn't a curse but a favor.

Finally, Paul says, **Be not overcome of evil, but overcome evil with good** (12:21).

CHAPTER 13
OBEDIENCE AND LOVE

Let every soul be subject unto the higher powers. For there is no power but of God: the powers that be are ordained of God (13:1). I accept this Scripture as the truth, but I don't always agree with God's choices of those in power.

God ordains some leaders who bungle the job badly. Such rulers become instruments to ripen a nation for judgment. Their mismanagement and injustices totally manifest the country's corruption so that no one questions God's judgment when it falls.

We know that our country needs judgment today, and we're being ripened for it. The deteriorating moral climate in the United States is reflected in the decisions made by our courts. Judicial decisions have been one of the greatest factors in opening the floodgates of corruption and immorality upon our land.

I believe that God has given our judges the power to make these landmark decisions. Because of this, I believe that He wants to bring judgment upon our immoral society, and He'll be blameless when He does.

When God told King Nebuchadnezzar of Babylon that his kingdom would fall to the Medo-Persian empire, the king built a ninety-foot golden image. He set up the statue in defiance of God's word and demanded that men worship it as a symbol of an eternal Babylon. "Is not this great Babylon that I have built for the house of the kingdom by the might of my power, and for the honour of my majesty?" (Daniel 4:30).

For these things God allowed Nebuchadnezzar to go insane. The king lived with the oxen for seven seasons. The dew of the heavens settled upon him, he ate grass in the fields, his nails grew like claws, and his hair like feathers covered his body—until he realized the truth. God in heaven establishes the kingdoms of men and puts in charge whomever He wishes.

Then Nebuchadnezzar made a proclamation about God. "He doeth according to his will in the army of heaven, and among the inhabitants of the earth: and none can stay his hand, or say unto him, What doest thou?" (Daniel 4:35). The king of Babylon came to his conclusion the difficult way. It's much easier just to believe that Romans 13:1 is true!

Whosoever therefore resisteth the power, resisteth the ordinance of God and they that resist shall receive unto themselves damnation. For rulers are not a terror to good works, but to the evil. Wilt thou then not be afraid of the power? do that which is good, and thou shalt have praise of the same (13:2-3). You don't need to fear the police as long as you obey the law. When you're traveling at the speed limit, you're not afraid. When you're traveling 25 miles-an-hour above the speed limit and pass a black-and-white car with a radar scanner in the side window, fear grips your heart.

Those who enforce the law aren't a threat or terror to you when you're obedient. Law-abiding citizens receive praise from the civil authorities. A police officer is only a terror to those who do evil works, **for he is the minister of God to thee for good** (13:4a). The next time you're stopped for speeding or violating the law, don't be nasty or angry. The officer may have saved your life. Be thankful for the police. If they weren't enforcing the laws, our society would be a much worse jungle than it is now.

But if thou do that which is evil, be afraid; for he beareth not the sword in vain: for he is the minister of God, a revenger to execute wrath upon him that doeth evil. Wherefore ye must needs be subject, not only for wrath, but also for conscience sake (13:4b-5). Be obedient to the law, not just because you're afraid of getting thrown in jail, but because of conscience.

For this cause pay ye tribute [taxes] also: for they are God's ministers, attending continually upon this very thing (13:6). Yes, they do "attend continually" on this very thing! Christians should pay their taxes. **Render therefore to all their dues: tribute to whom tribute is due; custom to whom custom** (13:7a). Pay the taxes, pay the customs. If you bought a taxable item in another country, don't try to sneak it in.

Give **fear to whom fear; honour to whom honour. Owe no man any thing, but to love one another: for he that loveth another hath fulfilled the law** (13:7b-8). Jesus said basically the same thing. The lawyer asked Him, "What is the greatest commandment?" Jesus replied, "Love the Lord your God with all your heart, soul, and mind, and love your neighbor as yourself. On these two commandments hang all the law" (Matthew 22:35, 40). The Law of God is simply summed up in love.

The Mosaic Law contained a negative note, "Thou shalt not..." (Deuteronomy 5:6-21). Jesus turned to a positive note: love God, love one another. We don't have to worry about the negatives.

Many people think that they're good because they don't do anything bad. It's much better to approach life with a positive attitude and let God's love flow through your heart. **For this, Thou shalt not commit adultery, Thou shalt not kill, Thou shalt not steal. Thou shalt not bear false witness, Thou shalt not covet; and if there be any other commandment, it is briefly comprehended in this saying, namely, Thou shalt love** (13:9). Once you have the positive, you can eliminate the negative. **Love worketh no ill to his neighbour: therefore love is the fulfilling of the law** (13:10). Everyone who loves has fulfilled the Law.

Now Paul gives the final thought of the chapter. **And that, knowing the time, that now it is high time to awake out of sleep** (13:11a). God doesn't want the coming of Christ to take you by surprise.

Jesus said, "Watch therefore: for ye know not what hour your Lord doth come. But know this, that if the goodman [owner] of the house had known in what watch the thief would come, he would have watched, and would not have suffered [allowed] his house to be broken up" (Matthew 24:42-43). He has given you the signs of His return, so it shouldn't catch you by surprise. For you're not children of "darkness, that that day should overtake you as a thief. Ye are all the children of light, and the children of the day" (I Thessalonians 5:4-5a). Therefore, "walk as children of light" (Ephesians 5:8b).

It's high time to wake up, look around at the world, and realize that this age is coming to an end. **For now is our salvation nearer than when we believed** (13:11b). Every day brings us that much closer to the return of Jesus Christ. **The night is far spent, the day is at hand** (13:12a). Satan has had control of the world since Adam turned it over to him, almost six thousand years ago. What a horrible night it's been!

Our nation has been corrupted by greed. Christopher Columbus believed that God was sending him as a light-bearer to a people in darkness. He wrote in his diary that the Holy Spirit led and directed his mission. When his crew saw the treasures of the Indians, the holy passion of reaching the natives for the Lord was turned into a lustful passion for gold. The explorers raped and murdered the Indians. Spain moved into Mexico, and so unfolded the horrible story of plundering, killing, and enslavement, all because of the greed for gold.

England's Jamestown colony was founded when English ministers encouraged their people to share the Gospel with the Indians in the New World. Again, greed overcame John Smith and his followers. The Indians were treated as inferiors, robbed, and murdered. The mission of the Jamestown community was doomed from the beginning.

Finally the Pilgrims came. They landed at Plymouth Rock and established the first successful colonization of the land. They shared the Gospel, made peace with the Indians, and maintained high moral standards. Their writings and the success of their colony prove that God's hand was upon them. Because these settlers were truly seeking to serve God, Plymouth Colony was a successful community.

On the first Thanksgiving Day the Pilgrims gave thanks to God for His care. Their provision hadn't been bountiful. During their first winter the daily ration of corn was five grains per person. However, God sustained them, and our nation was established on their religious and moral principles.

Today the term "Puritan" carries a negative connotation, but we need to be thankful for the puritan ethic established in America's early history. Were it not for these standards, our society would have collapsed long ago. When the light of the Gospel was fading in England and on the European Continent, God began to raise up

America as the new light of hope for all men. For a time
the light did shine. Unfortunately, the darkness is moving in once again, and America has become a home for
every kind of spiritual and moral blight. It's high time
that we awoke, for the "night is far spent." There are no
more frontiers to conquer where God can establish a new
light. The day is at hand when God will once again inter-
vene in the history of man.

**Let us therefore cast off the works of darkness,
and let us put on the armour of light. Let us walk
honestly, as in the day; not in rioting and drunken-
ness, not in chambering and wantonness [sexual
immorality and debauchery], not in strife and en-
vying** (13:12b-13). Let's live on life's positive side. **Let us
walk honestly... Put ye on the Lord Jesus Christ,
and make not provision for the flesh, to fulfil the
lusts thereof** (13:13a, 14). Don't gratify the desires of
your flesh. We need to be caring about the Lord's business. There's so much to be accomplished... and the time
is so short!

CHAPTER 14
JUDGING OTHERS

Paul now encourages us to receive those who are **weak in the faith... but not to doubtful disputations** (14:1). If a person is weak in the faith, receive him, but don't get into any big arguments.

It's tragic that in some churches a Christian must prove himself before he's received into the fellowship. Paul tells us to accept all people, whether they're spiritually mature or babes in Christ.

Paul gives two examples of believers weak in the faith: those who refuse to eat meat and those who insist on a particular day of worship. These Christians don't have enough faith to trust in the Lord completely. They feel that their righteousness still depends on keeping certain ordinances. You should love them, but don't debate these issues with them.

For one believeth that he may eat all things: another, who is weak in the faith eateth herbs [vegetables]. Let not him that eateth despise him that eateth not; and let not him which eateth not judge him that eateth: for God hath received him (14:2-3).

Different people have different convictions. A particular conviction may be good for one individual and wrong for another. God doesn't deal with us in the same ways, but meets us at our own levels. Some Christians have a strong conviction against going to public beaches and think that all Christians should avoid them. If going to a beach brings you problems of lust, then you shouldn't go. But you shouldn't set a universal Christian standard because of your own personal hang-up.

If God has convicted someone about eating meat, that person shouldn't eat meat. By the same token, he shouldn't assume that God has convicted everyone of the same thing and that anyone eating meat is a backslider. According to Paul, those who are weak in the faith eat vegetables; those who are strong in the faith eat anything. Paul said that all things are to be received with thanksgiving (Philippians 4:6). The New Testament prescribes no dietary restrictions as found in the Old Testament, and a Christian can eat pork or ham without violating any biblical precept.

If you have a strong conviction, don't judge those who lack it. Likewise, if you have no conviction, don't condemn those who are convicted. Simply accept and receive one another in love.

If you have an opinion on a Scripture that the rest of the church needs to know, then let them see how it works in your own life. As they see your belief conform you into the image of Christ, they'll be attracted to you. They'll approach you and ask questions. Then you'll have an opportunity to share your particular persuasion. Meanwhile, don't try to force your opinions on others or insist that they see things your way. The body of Christ needs to show greater latitude on these personal issues. Let's avoid divisions over the various ways we cross our 't's' and dot our 'i's'.

Who art thou that judgest another man's servant? to his own master he standeth or falleth (14:4a). We're not to judge one another because we're not the master. Every Christian belongs to God and serves Him. You have no business judging another man's servant. His own master will judge him, and before his master a servant stands or falls.

Yea, he shall be holden up: for God is able to make him stand (14:4b). Many people thought that I would never make it through Bible college, because I liked to get into mischief. However, they underestimated the power of God. He has sustained me and will continue to do so.

One man esteemeth one day above another (14:5a). Basically, men have esteemed two days for worship: Sabbath day (the "seventh day," from sundown Friday to sundown Saturday), and Sunday (the first day of the week). Please note that the Sabbath doesn't fall on Sunday.

The Jews and some churches observe the Sabbath as the holy day of the week. Unfortunately, some of these churches condemn those who don't observe the Sabbath. At one time the Seventh-day Adventist church taught that worshiping on Sunday was the same as taking the mark of the beast and anyone with the mark of the beast had no hope of salvation. So, worshiping God on Sunday instead of on Saturday was condemning yourself to hell. I'm so thankful that God is broader than the narrowness of man. If our salvation was predicated on the concepts of man, none of us would make it. (Fortunately, some in the Seventh-day Adventist church have since modified their position.)

The Book of Acts records that Christians gathered to break bread on the first day of the week, Sunday (Acts 20:7). Paul told the Corinthians to bring their offerings together on the first day of the week (I Corinthians 16:2). Some of the early Church historians wrote about gathering to worship on Sunday. For example, Tertullian noted that many believers felt they should only break bread together on the first day of the week because Christ arose on that day.

Many who religiously observe the Sabbath claim that Sunday worship is linked with the Babylonian corruption of the Church during the time of Constantine. However, the practice of Sunday worship began long before Constantine.

Another esteemeth every day alike. Let every man be fully persuaded in his own mind (14:5b). Some people regard Sunday as a holy day and so refrain from certain activities on that day. Others regard every day as a day of worship, and to them Sunday isn't above another day.

Personally, I consider every day alike. My wife wishes that I'd be more observant of birthdays and anniversaries, but I esteem every day as the Lord's day, and I do the Lord's business. I don't say, "Today is the Lord's day and the rest of the week is mine." All my days belong to Him.

He that regardeth the day, regardeth it unto the Lord (14:6a). If you regard the Sabbath day, you're regarding it unto the Lord. **And he that regardeth not the day, to the Lord he doth not regard it** (14:6b). If you don't regard a particular day, then you're regarding every day as unto the Lord.

He that eateth, eateth to the Lord, for he giveth God thanks; and he that eateth not, to the Lord he eateth not, and giveth God thanks (14:6c). Whether we eat meat or abstain from meat and eat vegetables, we thank God for our food.

For none of us liveth to himself, and no man dieth to himself (14:7). We all have an influence on other people. We don't live in isolation chambers.

For whether we live, we live unto the Lord; and whether we die, we die unto the Lord: whether we live therefore, or die, we are the Lord's. For to this end Christ both died, and rose, and revived, that he might be Lord both of the dead and living. But why dost thou judge thy brother? or why dost thou set at nought thy brother? for we shall all stand before the judgment seat of Christ (14:8-10).

We're not to judge one another. To "set at nought thy brother" is to declare that he isn't a Christian because of what he does. "He can't be a Christian because he worships on Sunday instead of on the Sabbath." We shouldn't judge our brothers, because one day we'll all stand before the judgment seat of Christ. "We must all appear before the judgment seat of Christ; that every one may receive the things done in his body... whether it be good or bad" (II Corinthians 5: 10). As we stand before Jesus Christ to be judged, the standard by which we'll be judged is the same we use to judge others. He told us, "Judge not, that you be not judged. For with what judgment you judge, you will be judged" (Matthew 7:1-2).

A Christian is never under any condemnation. "There is therefore now no condemnation to them which are in Christ Jesus" (Romans 8:1a). However, several types of judgments are found in the Scriptures. There is the believer's self-judgment. Paul tells us to examine ourselves when we come to the Lord's table. "For if we would judge ourselves, we should not be judged" (1 Corinthians 11:31).

There will also be the judgment of the believer before the judgment seat of Christ (14:10b). This is the bema seat, equivalent to the judge's seat in the Olympic Games. After each game, the winners came before the judge's seat to receive crowns for first, second, and third places. Likewise, the Christian's works will be tested by fire, and he'll be rewarded for those which remain. If the fire consumes all his works, he won't receive a reward, but he'll be saved "yet so as by fire" (I Corinthians 3:15). The judgment seat of Christ is only concerned with a Christian's rewards and position in the kingdom, not with his salvation.

The Lord will judge our works by our motives. What motivates us to serve the Lord? Are we looking for recognition from men? Jesus said, "Take heed that ye do not your alms [acts of righteousness] before men, to be seen of them" (Matthew 6:1a). If your motive is to be seen of man, then Jesus said, "You have your reward" (Matthew 6:2). Unfortunately, the praises of men are a powerful motivation, and much Christian work is done for such psychological reasons.

For it is written, As I live, saith the Lord, every knee shall bow to me, and every tongue shall confess to God (14:11). Paul also quotes this verse from Isaiah 45:23 in Philippians. Christ emptied himself and was "obedient unto death, even the death of the cross. Wherefore God also hath highly exalted him, and given him a name which is above every name: that at the name of Jesus every knee should bow... and that every tongue should confess that Jesus Christ is Lord, to the glory of God the Father" (Philippians 2:8b-11).

So then every one of us shall give account of himself to God (14:12). All will give an account of themselves before God. I'll be responsible for the things that I've done, and you'll be responsible for what you've done. I won't account for you, nor will you account for me.

Let us not therefore judge one another any more: but judge this rather, that no man put a stumbling-block or an occasion to fall in his brother's way (14:13). We stumble a weaker brother by flaunting our freedom in Christ before him. He may be emboldened to follow our example. Yet when he does, he offends his own conscience and is thereby stumbled. Let's do everything possible to avoid stumbling our brothers.

I know, and am persuaded by the Lord Jesus, that there is nothing unclean of itself: but to him that esteemeth any thing to be unclean, to him it is unclean (14:14). That's a powerful statement. Paul knows that nothing of itself is unclean. He could eat pork without any pangs of conscience. Jesus said, "It isn't what goes into a man's mouth that defiles a man" (Matthew 15:17-20).

Peter saw a sheet come down from heaven with both clean and unclean animals. The Lord said, "Rise, Peter. Kill and eat" He replied, "Lord, I've never eaten any unclean food". Jesus said, "Don't call that unclean which I have cleansed." This happened to Peter three times (Acts 10:9-16). Though the main significance of the vision was that the Gospel would be preached to the Gentiles, it also showed that nothing is unclean of itself. All things are to "be received with thanksgiving" (I Timothy 4:4).

Still, if I consider something to be unclean, then for me it is unclean. Why? Because my relationship to God is based upon faith.

Many things can hinder my faith, and one of the greatest hindrances is sin. Satan uses my sins to accuse me, condemn me, and keep me from those things God wants to give me. Satan points out my failures and weaknesses, claiming that I'm worthless in God's sight. Since I've been conditioned to believe that good boys are rewarded and bad boys are punished, it's difficult to believe that God would bless me unless I deserve it. Yet, God doesn't bless me on the basis of my goodness. He blesses me on the basis of His grace and love for me.

If I believe something to be true, then to me it becomes true. If I believe that God can't bless me because of my conduct, then I can't be blessed of God. Unfortunately, some people regard God's blessings as approval for all their actions, and that's dangerous. If God blesses me, He does so on the basis of my belief in Him, and I'm receiving by faith. God doesn't withhold His blessings from me every time I fail or stumble, but neither do His blessings necessarily mean He approves of my life-style.

Sadly, there's been a great deal of preaching against so-called unclean things. In some circles a person's salvation is questioned if he smokes cigarettes. A Christian can smoke cigarettes or even cigars and not affect his relationship with God in the least. Despite this truth, many people are lost due to their cigarette habit. They've tried to give up smoking, but failed. Because they've been taught that they can't be Christians as long as they smoke, they don't believe that God has washed and cleansed them from their sins. Thus, their belief becomes a tragic reality.

One day a man came to me and said, "Chuck, I'd like to be a Christian. I believe in God and I'd love to go to church. But I need a can of beer when I get home. I work hard and it relaxes me". I asked him, "Who told you that you couldn't have a can of beer?" This man had a conviction against beer and considered it unclean. It kept him from true fellowship with God and from attending church. The Lord doesn't demand that we clean up our lives before coming to Him. He invites us to come just as we are—ungodly, unrighteous sinners. He accepts us as we are, then begins His work of transforming us into His image.

The Bible teaches us to be moderate in all things, and there are limits to our liberty. We shouldn't exercise our liberty so it brings us into bondage. A fellow who needs beer just to relax isn't a free person, even if a Christian. Anytime you're under the power of a thing, you're no longer free. Some people are under the control of a sport, such as surfing, water-skiing, or tennis. They go out to surf, but if the waves are small their day is ruined. Instead, I say, "Praise the Lord! Let's go jogging!" I love my freedom in Jesus Christ, and I wouldn't trade it for anything.

But if thy brother be grieved with thy meat [freedom], now walkest thou not charitably. Destroy not him with your meat, for whom Christ died (14:15). Paul gives us an important rule here. You have your freedom, but don't exercise it in front of a weak brother and stumble him. The work of Christ can be negated in an immature believer when you flaunt your freedom before him.

Let not then your good be evil spoken of (14:16). You're free to do many things. However, others may not understand this and will speak evil of you, because you're boasting of your liberty.

For the kingdom of God is not meat and drink (14:17a). The kingdom of God isn't a matter of what you can or cannot eat. Unfortunately, the rules of eating and drinking have become a major issue of the kingdom. But the kingdom of God is **righteousness, and peace, and joy in the Holy Ghost** (14:17b). Christians who are hung up about eating and drinking are roaming in the spiritual wilderness. They haven't entered the real kingdom, the fullness of God's Spirit with His glorious peace and joy.

For he that in these things serveth Christ is acceptable to God, and approved of men (14:18). God accepts you and men approve of you when you walk in the Spirit, filled with the peace and joy of God. Instead of stumbling people, you're a blessing to them.

Let us therefore follow after the things which make for peace, and things wherewith one may edify [build up] another (14:19). Let's do things that bring us together as a body rather than divide us. Let's build up one another in the faith, especially the weaker brethren.

For meat destroy not the work of God (14:20a). Because you feel free to eat pork chops, don't destroy the work of God in some sensitive fellow, such as a Seventh-day Adventist who may be a vegetarian. He's also a Christian and loves the Lord. Don't argue with him about eating meat.

I have some wonderful Seventh-day Adventist friends, including a dentist who would take advantage of me. He'd get me in the chair, prop open my mouth with hardware, and then talk to me. I listened because I had to. I still respect his opinion and consider him a friend to this day. I accept him as a Christian brother, though I don't share his views. I expect to see him in heaven, but I think he'll be surprised to see me there!

All things indeed are pure; but it is evil for that man who eateth with offence (14:20b). You can do a right thing in a wrong way. Your action may be all right, but you can do it offensively, and that is an act of evil. You're destroying the work of Christ in a person instead of building him up in love.

It is good neither to eat flesh, nor to drink wine, nor any thing whereby thy brother stumbleth, or is offended, or is made weak (14:21). If certain things offend or weaken my brother, I won't do them in front of him. Christian love causes me to live with more restraint than my own convictions demand. I gladly deny myself so as not to offend or stumble a weaker brother.

Hast thou faith [faith to eat meat without a guilty conscience]? have it to thyself before God. Happy is he that condemneth not himself in that thing which he alloweth (14:22). You're a happy man when your heart doesn't condemn you. Liberty in Christ has set you free from all bondage.

And he that doubteth is damned if he eat, because he eateth not of faith: for whatsoever is not of faith is sin (14:23). It's wrong to talk someone out of his convictions. When a person is pressured to act against his convictions, he feels condemned before God. His conscience will whip him, and Satan will take full advantage of his feelings. He'll try to make the weaker brother feel alienated from God. Be wary of becoming an unwitting tool in Satan's hands by urging a brother to act against his convictions. Let everyone serve God according to his own measure of faith.

CHAPTER 15
CHRISTIAN UNITY

We then that are strong [strong in the faith] ought to bear the infirmities of the weak, and not to please ourselves (15:1). Your faith may be strong. Great! Use it to hold up the weaker brothers, not to please yourself. Your concern should always be to help others.

Let everyone of us please his neighbor for his good to edification. For even Christ pleased not himself; but, as it is written, The reproaches of them that reproached thee fell on me (15:2-3). Christ took upon Himself the reproaches aimed at God, because He didn't live to please Himself. In like manner, we take upon ourselves the reproaches directed against Christ. Many times we're reproached for being too narrow or restrictive, because we seek to deny our flesh to walk after Christ. Jesus set the example for us of living not to please ourselves. If we seek in all things to please God, we'll never go wrong.

For whatsoever things were written aforetime were written for our learning, that we through patience and comfort of the scriptures might have hope (15:4). The Scriptures were written for our learning, so we would have hope through their message of patience and comfort. Paul prayed for the Ephesians that God would open their eyes of understanding, that they might know the hope of their calling (Ephesians 1:18). If we only understood all that God has in store for us in His eternal kingdom, we would gladly sacrifice to deny our flesh now for the hope of that glorious future with Him.

Now the God of patience and consolation grant you to be likeminded one toward another according to Christ Jesus: that ye may with one mind and one mouth glorify God, even the Father of our Lord Jesus Christ. Wherefore receive ye one another, as Christ also received us to the glory of God (15:5-7). We should strive for unity of mind and heart, receiving one another and accepting our differences within the body of Christ. Differences do exist, but they need not divide us into splinter groups. We can accept one another in love, because Christ has received us all. This accepting love marks true spiritual maturity.

Now I say that Jesus Christ was a minister of the circumcision for the truth of God, to confirm the promises made unto the fathers (15:8). Jesus ministered to the Jews, the "circumcision," to fulfill God's promises to these people. When He first sent out His disciples, He said, "Don't go into the cities of the Gentiles" (Matthew 10:5). When the Gentile woman came to Jesus about her possessed daughter, He said, "I'm only sent to the lost sheep of the house of Israel" (Matthew 15:24). Christ came to fulfill the promises God made to the Jewish nation.

And that the Gentiles might glorify God for his mercy; as it is written, For this cause I will confess to thee among the Gentiles, and sing unto thy name. And again he saith, Rejoice, ye Gentiles, with his people. And again, Praise the Lord, all ye Gentiles; and laud him, all ye people. And again Isaiah saith, There shall be a root of Jesse, and he that shall rise to reign over the Gentiles (15:9-12a). The prophet Isaiah foretold that the Messiah would reign over the Gentiles.

Although Jesus ministered to the Jews in fulfillment of the promises of God, He opened the way for all to receive the forgiveness of their sins. Through His death and resurrection, the Gentiles have been brought into the mercies of God. **In Him shall the Gentiles trust** (15:12b).

Now the God of hope fill you with all joy and peace in believing—this peace comes by believing in the Lord—**that ye may abound in hope, through the power of the Holy Ghost** (15:13). As Paul closes his letter, he ministers with benedictions and prayers for his readers.

And I myself also am persuaded of you, my brethren, that ye also are full of goodness, filled with all knowledge, able also to admonish one another (15:14). The word "admonish" would better read "effectively minister" or "competently instruct." As Christians, we should be ministering God's truth to one another in love.

Nevertheless, brethren, I have written the more boldly unto you in some sort, as putting you in mind, because of the grace that is given to me of God, that I should be the minister of Jesus Christ to the Gentiles, ministering the gospel of God, that the offering up of the Gentiles might be acceptable, being sanctified by the Holy Ghost (15:15-16). Paul speaks of his ministry to the Gentiles and his hope that their offerings, praises, and worship through the Holy Spirit might be acceptable to God.

I have therefore whereof I may glory through Jesus Christ in those things which pertain to God. For I will not dare to speak of any of those things which Christ hath not wrought by me, to make the Gentiles obedient, by word and deed, through mighty signs and wonders, by the power of the Spirit of God; so that from Jerusalem and round

about into Illyricum, I have fully preached the gospel of Christ (15:17-19). Paul's ministry to the Gentiles was confirmed through the signs and by the power of the Holy Spirit.

The Jews believed that a Gentile could only be saved by proselytizing and becoming a Jew. The idea that God wanted to save the Gentiles was inconceivable. However, the power of the Holy Spirit soon changed the minds of the Hebrew Christians. When the church in Jerusalem gathered together to discuss the Gentiles, Peter testified. "And as I began to speak, the Holy Ghost fell on them, as on us at the beginning" (Acts 11:15). The work of the Holy Spirit on the Gentiles proved that God would save them, too (Acts 11:18).

Then Paul testified of the miracles that God had worked upon the Gentiles. The miracles confirmed that the Gentiles had received God's Word. Paul speaks of "fully preaching" the Gospel of Christ among the Gentiles (15:19), because it was accompanied by many signs and wonders by the Holy Spirit. The miracles of healing in the early Church were signs to the unbelievers confirming the truths declared by the followers of Jesus Christ. Miracles weren't limited to the apostles, as they also accompanied the ministries of Philip (Acts 8:6), Stephen (Acts 6:8), and others.

Yea, so have I strived to preach the gospel, not where Christ was named, lest I should build upon another man's foundation (15:20). Commendably, Paul didn't try to take over where someone else had started. He went to preach the Gospel where it hadn't been heard yet. As a result, Paul converted many people to Christ and discipled them. There were others who would then follow him around and seek to turn the new believers from Paul and his teaching. These men challenged Paul's apostleship and taught their own pernicious doctrines.

They wouldn't evangelize but fed off the work of others. The same is true today. Many men go around with a message for the Church, bringing their false doctrines to the established body rather than going to the lost.

But as it is written, To whom he was not spoken of, they shall see: and they that have not heard shall understand. For which cause also I have been much hindered from coming to you. But now having no more place in these parts, and having a great desire these many years to come unto you; whensoever I take my journey into Spain, I will come to you: for I trust to see you in my journey, and to be brought on my way thitherward by you, if first I be somewhat filled with your company (15:21-24).

Paul here writes on a more familiar level to the Roman Christians, expressing his personal desire to see them. At the time of this writing, Paul was delivering a gift from the Gentile believers to the saints in Jerusalem. He wasn't exactly sure about this visit to Jerusalem, for the Holy Spirit was warning him that bonds and imprisonment awaited him there (Acts 21:11).

Whether or not Paul ever went to Spain is a matter of conjecture. Certain legends tell of him preaching the Gospel in that land. These stories have never been confirmed and may simply spring from verse 24 in Romans 15.

Paul did journey to Rome as the result of his appeal to Caesar, when Festus was seeking to use him as a political pawn. He arrived in Rome under guard, but the believers in Rome came out to greet him. Paul had a powerful and effective ministry there, even though a prisoner.

But now I go unto Jerusalem to minister unto the saints (15:25). Paul's ministry included bringing an offering to the believers. **For it hath pleased them of Macedonia and Achaia to make a certain contribution for the poor saints which are at Jerusalem** (15:26). The saints of

Jerusalem, who thought the Lord was coming back very soon, sold their possessions and placed the money into one common fund. When the money ran out, they were in a financial crisis. Paul took an offering among the Gentiles as an example of their love for them. As a pastor of a Gentile congregation, I find it thrilling to take offerings for the Jews in Israel as a witness for Jesus Christ. How wonderful to shock these people with our love for them and by not asking for anything in return.

It hath pleased them verily; and their debtors they are (15:27a). I don't know by what standard the Gentiles owed the gift to the Jerusalem church, yet Paul understood the situation that way.

For if the Gentiles have been made partakers of their spiritual things, their duty is also to minister unto them in carnal things (15:27b). When he wrote to the Corinthians, Paul told them to minister to the physical needs of their spiritual teachers. "For it is written in the law of Moses, thou shalt not muzzle the mouth of the ox that treadeth out the corn" (I Corinthians 9:9).

When therefore I have performed this, and have sealed to them this fruit, I will come by you [on my way] into Spain. And I am sure that, when I come unto you, I shall come in the fulness of the blessing of the gospel of Christ (15:28-29). Paul didn't realize that he'd soon enter Rome as a prisoner, but he did know that he'd come in the fullness of the Gospel of Christ. That's the only way Paul ever traveled!

Now I beseech you, brethren, for the Lord Jesus Christ's sake, and for the love of the Spirit, that ye strive together with me in your prayers to God for me (15:30). Paul requests that the believers agonize and strive in their prayers. The Greek word for "strive" in verse 30 is translated "press" in Philippians: "I press towards the mark for the prize of the high calling of God in Christ Jesus" (Philippians 3:14). Paul begs them to pray strenuously and with perseverance for him. "Put everything you've got into those prayers!"

Ministers need the prayers of their flocks. With Paul I urge you to strive in your prayers for your pastors. We need your prayers and we thank God for them. Pastors are sustained by the power of the Spirit through the prayer support of their congregations.

That I may be delivered from them that do not believe in Judea; and that my service which I have for Jerusalem may be accepted of the saints; that I may come unto you with joy by the will of God, and may with you be refreshed (15:31-32). Paul asked the Romans to pray for three things. First, that he might be delivered from the unbelieving Jews. This petition was answered in an unusual way. When Paul was in the temple in Jerusalem, some of the Asian Jews reported that he had brought Gentiles into the temple grounds and had been teaching against Moses. This excited the crowd, and they grabbed Paul and sought to beat him to death. The Roman guard rushed into the melee and rescued him (Acts 21:29-32). So, Paul was delivered from the unbelieving Jews.

The second prayer request was answered when the church in Jerusalem received his offering. His third request, to come to Rome, was fulfilled, but not as Paul had anticipated.

Now the God of peace be with you all. Amen (15:33).

CHAPTER 16
BLESSINGS

In Chapter 16 Paul sends his personal greetings to the church in Rome. We won't comment on all the names in this chapter, but we'll call your attention to a few of special interest.

I commend unto you Phoebe our sister, which is a servant of the church which is in Cenchrea (16:1). This word "servant" in the Greek means "deaconess". The deacons and deaconesses of the early Church cared for the church's material needs. Phoebe, a deaconess, carried Paul's letter to the Roman believers. Paul calls her a "sister" and commends her to them, **that ye receive her in the Lord, as becometh saints, and that ye assist her in whatsoever business she has need of you: for she hath been a succourer [helper] of many, and of myself also** (16:2). Phoebe, a faithful sister in Christ, helped Paul very much. Women have always played a great role in the body of Christ.

Greet Priscilla and Aquila my helpers in Christ Jesus (16:3) Priscilla and Aquila were tent-makers who had left Rome under the persecution of Claudius (A.D. 41-54). Paul, also a tent-maker, met and worked with them on his first visit to Corinth. The couple then moved from Corinth to Ephesus. When Apollos came there to preach, they took him aside and explained the Word of God more completely to him (Acts 18:26). They also ministered with Paul in Ephesus. At the time of this epistle, they were back in Rome.

Wherever Priscilla and Aquila went they shared the Gospel. They were like the Christian couples of today who move into a new neighborhood, open their homes, and start Bible studies. So Paul says, **Greet the church that is in their house** (16:5a). People gathered in their house to study the Word of God. The Church of Jesus Christ can meet in a home, on a field, or on board a ship. His Church is made up of people who love Him and are united by His Spirit. It meets whenever Christians gather to study the Word, praise the Lord, and edify one another.

Speaking of Priscilla and Aquila, Paul said, **Who have for my life laid down their own necks; unto whom not only I give thanks, but also all the churches of the Gentiles** (16:4). This husband and wife team proved to be a real blessing to the Gentile churches. They must have been an outstanding couple, and I look forward to meeting them in heaven.

Paul continues to send more greetings. **Salute Andronicus and Junia, my kinsmen, and my fellow prisoners, who are of note among the apostles, who also were in Christ before me** (16:7). Since Junia is a feminine name, there are two possible interpretations of this verse. (1) Junia was known and respected by Peter and John, who were apostles before Paul. (2) Junia was an apostle and, thus, there were women apostles in the early Church. It's impossible to be dogmatic about either interpretation, but the Greek language of the text appears to support the latter.

The role of women in the early Church was important. Many women today find fault with Paul, because he told the women of Corinth to keep silent in church (I Corinthians 14:34). Let's look at his statement in context. Paul didn't say that women were never to speak in church. In an earlier chapter he had given them instructions about prophesying and praying in the church (I Corinthians 11).

Most of the early churches started in synagogues, where men sat on one side and women on the other. The Jews didn't allow men and women to sit together during the services. Today, a wife can nudge her husband and ask, "What does the pastor mean?" In Corinth a woman had to call across the room to ask her husband about the sermon. So, Paul told the women to keep silent and wait until they returned home to question their husbands.

Paul esteemed women as highly as men. Here in Romans 16:7 he greets his "kinsmen," including a woman, Junia, possibly a noted apostle in Christ before him.

Salute one another with an holy kiss. The churches of Christ salute you (16:16). When I visited a church in Rome a few years ago, the men greeted me with a holy kiss. I thought it appropriate that the church in Rome still greets the brethren with a holy kiss, as Paul instructed here.

Now I beseech you, brethren, mark them which cause divisions and offences that are contrary to the doctrine which ye have learned; and avoid them (16:17). We're to accept differences regarding diet, holy days, and other such customs, but we must draw the line with important doctrines. One of the greatest dangers within a church isn't the exercise of liberty by believers, but the false doctrines brought in by deceivers.

For they that are such serve not our Lord Jesus Christ, but their own belly; and by good words and fair speeches deceive the hearts of the simple (16:18). Through eloquent speeches, clever sayings, and novel ideas these men deceive those who lack a proper understanding of the Word of God.

The Church across the United States, especially among the charismatic groups, has been recently divided by various damnable doctrines. These include the doctrine of shepherding (in which a person must submit to the authority of a "shepherd" who is responsible to God for him) and the doctrine that Christians can be possessed by demons and must have them cast out.

The latest and most pernicious of all these false doctrines is that a Christian's lack of health or wealth is a sign of his lack of faith. This doctrine proclaims that it's never God's will for a believer to suffer. This false concept receiving such a wide audience today didn't come from God's Word but from Christian Science and Science of Mind. They teach the same basic concept: what you say is what you'll get. These doctrines have divided the body of Christ, and we're told to mark those who spread them.

Referring to the Christians in Rome, Paul continues, **For your obedience [to the Word and to Christ] is come abroad unto all men. I am glad therefore on your behalf: but yet I would have you wise unto that which is good, and simple concerning evil** (16:19). Paul wants us to be wise in good things and simple in evil things. Don't probe into the work of Satan or seek understanding about witchcraft, the occult, or the evils of today. The Lord warned His people in the Old Testament not to study how the heathen worshiped their gods (Deuteronomy 12:30). Be ignorant of evil, but be wise in the good, righteous, and wonderful truths of the Spirit.

And the God of peace shall bruise Satan under your feet shortly (16:20a). God prophesied to Adam and Eve that the serpent (Satan) would bruise the

Messiah's heel, but the seed of the woman (the Messiah) would bruise his head (Genesis 3:15). No doubt referring to that prophecy, Paul said that God would "bruise Satan under your feet shortly." This event hasn't happened yet. Satan still wields power on earth, walking about as a roaring lion (I Peter 5:8). God will deal with him soon, and he'll be bound and cast into the abyss. Take heart, because we're near that time!

The grace of our Lord Jesus Christ be with you. Amen. Timotheus my workfellow, and Lucius, and Jason, and Sosipater, my kinsmen, salute you (16:20b-21).

The scribe to whom Paul dictated this letter gives his own greeting. **I Tertius, who wrote this epistle, salute you in the Lord. Gaius mine host, and of the whole church, saluteth you. Erastus the chamberlain of the city saluteth you, and Quartus a brother. The grace of our Lord Jesus Christ be with you all. Amen** (16:22-24).

Paul begins his final benediction to the church in Rome. **Now to him that is of power to stablish you according to my gospel, and the preaching of Jesus Christ, according to the revelation of the mystery, which was kept secret since the world began, but now is made manifest, and by the scriptures of the prophets, according to the commandment of the everlasting God, made known to all nations for the obedience of faith: to God only wise, be glory through Jesus Christ for ever. Amen** (16:25-27).

Paul speaks of the "revelation of the mystery" (16:25). A mystery in Scripture isn't a truth that was difficult to understand. Rather, it's a truth that wasn't revealed by the Spirit until these latter days. Paul speaks much of such mysteries in his Epistle to the Ephesians.

I don't believe that the Spirit is revealing any new mysteries today. God has already given us His wonderful revelation of all that pertains to life and godliness. We don't need new truths. We need new experience in the truths God has made known in the Book of Romans and throughout His eternal Word. Amen!

APPENDIX
STUDY GUIDE
INTRODUCTION

The New Testament is divided into three categories. The first contains the Gospels, the first four books of the New Testament, which deal with the life of Christ. Next is the Book of Acts, which continues Christ's ministry through His apostles. The rest of the New Testament is made up of epistles, which are concerned with matters of doctrine. Romans is the first epistle.

In determining scriptural conduct for the Church, we use hermeneutics, or scriptural interpretation, as our guide. If something was taught by Christ, practiced in Acts, and taught in the Epistles, then we feel that it can be properly practiced by the Church .

ROMANS 1: THE LOST WORLD

v.1 "Servant" means "bondslave." The slave was completely at his master's disposal. His one goal in life was to serve.

"Apostle" means "one who is sent." Paul was called to be an apostle and sent by the Holy Spirit to witness to the Gentiles.

"Gospel" means "good news."

v.2 The message of the Gospel was promised in the Old Testament.

v.3 The name Jesus is the Greek word for Joshua, which in Hebrew means "Jehovah is salvation."

Christ is Greek for the Hebrew word "Messiah" which means "Anointed One."

Jesus is His name, Christ is His distinction, and Lord is His title, signifying our relationship with Him.

Mary was a descendant of David, to whom God had made the promise that Messiah would come through him.

v.7 All those in the body of Christ are saints. After we experience the grace of God and make our peace with Him, we can know the peace of God in every situation.

v.11 Paul's desire to go to Rome was to minister to the church there.

v.14 "Barbarians" refers to those who didn't speak Greek. They weren't necessarily wild, coarse people as the name implies today.

v.16 This verse speaks of the power of God.

v.17 This verse speaks of the righteousness of God and introduces the theme of this epistle: righteousness comes by faith, not by works.

v.18 This verse speaks of the wrath of God. Ungodly means "not in the right relationship with God." Unrighteous means "not in the right relationship with man". We cannot have the proper relationship with God and have the wrong relationship with man. Holding the truth in unrighteousness is believing that there is a God, yet living as though He didn't exist.

v.20 We can see God in His creation.

v.21 I Thessalonians 5:18; Psalm 37:23; Romans 8:28.

v.23 The idols which men create often look like grotesque forms of men and beasts.

v.24-28 When men create their own god, they become like the god they serve and rapidly degenerate. God gives them up to their own base desire. Homosexuality is the result of moral depravity; people are not "born" homosexuals but have been given up to their own lusts.

v.29-31 Our society has sought to rule God out of its conscience and now evidences the evils of reprobate minds.

v.32 Movies and television programs that glorify lying, cheating, stealing, murder, and adultery can cause us to take pleasure in these sins and make us guilty.

ROMANS 2: GOD'S JUSTICE

v.2 God will not only judge a person's actions but also his motivations. He knows the truth about each of us.

v.4 People mistake God's mercy and long-suffering for weakness or indifference to their sin and rebellion. God's goodness, not the threat of judgment and hell, leads a man to repentance.

v.6 We ask for God's mercy, not justice; for our sins deserve punishment.

v.11 God will judge us without regard to our nationality.

v.12-15 We'll be judged according to the knowledge that we have. God has given every man a conscience, so that he knows good and evil.

v.17-29 Rituals will not save us if we're not walking according to God's will, whether we're circumcised, baptized, or members of a church. Obedience to God, not rituals, counts for salvation.

ROMANS 3: THE FREE GIFT

v.2 The Word of God was given to the Jews, who preserved the Scriptures with diligence and accuracy.

v.3 Our belief in God doesn't add to Him, nor does our unbelief detract from Him.

v.5 Since God has said that all men have sinned, some people say they sin to prove that God spoke the truth. This is evil reasoning.

v.7 Some people tell untrue stories to sway people's emotions and bring them to salvation, but this is wrong.

v.10-18 Every man is guilty before God. There's not one man who dares to stand before God in his own righteousness.

v.20 No man can be justified by keeping the Law. The Law was intended to show us our sin, not to justify us. "Justified" means "just as if I never did it."

v.21-22 There was a righteousness apart from the Law that was spoken of in the Old Testament. This righteousness was the justification through faith in God's grace and mercy. Our salvation is based on God's faithfulness rather than the variability of our goodness.

v.23 We all have sinned, some more than others; but all of us have fallen short of the goal God has for us.

v.24-26 God has a righteous basis for our justification through the sacrifice of Jesus for our sins.

v.27 All we have done to gain salvation is to believe in the salvation God provided for us.

v.31 The Law is established because it has done its work of showing us our sin and driving us to the redemption we have in Jesus.

ROMANS 4: ABRAHAM AND FAITH

v.1 What did Abraham discover?

v.2 Abraham didn't trust in his works to save him (Romans 7:18).

v.3 God imputes righteousness to us when we believe Him.

v.4-5 If we try to approach God on the basis of our works, we nullify His grace. When we have a right relationship with God, our natural response that flows from our hearts is to do anything He wants us to. Our works are thus motivated by love (2 Corinthians 5:14).

v.7 "Blessed" means "Oh, how happy!"

v.9-11 God considered Abraham righteous before he had ever been circumcised.

v.13-14 Abraham was accounted righteous before the Law was ever given.

v.15 There is no way to break a law before it exists.

v.16 Our salvation is not variable, i.e., dependent on our works, but is as sure as God's promise to us.

v.17 God talked about Abraham's son as if Isaac existed before he was even conceived.

v.18-21 The four keys to Abraham's faith:

(1) Abraham ignored the human possibilities and trusted to God to keep His promises (Isaiah 55:8, 9).

(2) Abraham did not stagger at the promises of God (Philippians 4:19).

(3) Abraham praised God before the evidence was there.

(4) Abraham believed God was able to do what He had said He would (Isaiah 40:15; Ephesians 3:20).

ROMANS 5: JUST AS IF I NEVER DID IT

v.2 We have access to the Father any time our righteousness is based on faith. When our righteousness is based on our keeping the Law, access to the Father depends on our works.

v.3 The trials that come into our lives promote spiritual growth.

v.6-8 Christ died for sinners, not "righteous" people (Mark 2:17).

v.9-10 Christ died for us when we were sinners and reconciled us to God. Now He establishes our relationship with God through His life.

v.11 The word "atonement" in the Old Testament meant "covering." The blood of the sacrifice covered the sins of the people, but it couldn't put away their sins. In the New Testament, "atonement" means "at one-ment," because Christ's death put away our sins and made us one with Him.

v.12-14 When Adam sinned he brought sin into the world, and every man after him was born a sinner.

v.15 One man brought sin into the world, and one Man died for the forgiveness of the world's sins.

v.18 Adam's sin brought condemnation on us; Christ's death bought justification for us.

ROMANS 6: VICTORY OVER SIN

v.2 "God forbid" means "perish the thought." When we're born again, our spirits are put in control of our bodies and minds. In the spiritual dimension, we fellowship with God and are conscious of Him.

v.3-4 We buried the old flesh-dominated nature in baptism, and the new creature is free from sin.

v.6 "Destroyed" is katargeo which means "to put out of business. " This should read in the past tense, "Our old man was crucified."

v.11 God didn't intend for our bodily appetites to rule over us, but, as long as we're in these bodies, we'll have a struggle with the flesh. We must daily go before God to reckon our old nature dead and by faith to claim the victory (Galatians 5).

v.12-13 We don't have to sin anymore. We now have the choice to yield to the flesh or to God.

v.14-17 We've been freed from being servants of sin. Now that we're free from the bondage of sin and are under grace, it doesn't make sense to sin. Instead, we can yield ourselves to God as His instruments for righteousness.

v.21 The fruit (or product) of sin is death.

v.22-23 The fruit of holiness is eternal life.

ROMANS 7: FLESH VS. SPIRIT

v.1 When Paul uses the word "brethren" he's referring to his Jewish brothers. The principle Paul begins to establish here is that death brings freedom from the Law.

v.4-6 The Jews who had become Christians thought they still had to keep the Law. So, Paul explained that they had died in Christ. Once freed from the Law, we can serve God from the motivation of love.

v.7 Paul here states that the purpose of the Law was to show men their sins.

v.14 We're in agreement with the Law because it is good and just. Our problem is that the Law is spiritual and we are carnal. Jesus explained God's intention when He gave the Law, because the Pharisees had misinterpreted it (Matthew 5-7). The New Covenant we have with God depends upon our belief in His righteousness. The Old Covenant depended on our righteousness in keeping the Law.

v.15 This is the struggle Paul had before he realized that the Law was spiritual.

v.17-20 Only the Christian has this conflict between the flesh and the spirit. The non-Christian lives in harmony with the desires of his flesh, but we Christians are trying to bring our flesh into conformity with the will of God. Now our will and desire is to serve God. So, when we sin, it's because we still have the sinful nature.

v.22 My spiritual, inward self loves God's law and wants above all to obey Him.

v.23 Our flesh always seeks to gratify itself and struggles with our spirit to bring it under the control of sin.

v.24 We're dragging the body of our dead man (our flesh) around with us, hoping for the day when we'll be released.

v.25 With God's help through Jesus, there's a way that we don't have to continue to be defeated by the flesh.

ROMANS 8: SET FREE!

v.1 Because in our hearts we desire to serve God, He doesn't condemn us when we fail.

v.2 The law of sin and death is still in effect, but the new law of life in Christ Jesus supersedes the old Law.

v.3-4 The law of sin and death couldn't make us righteous, but the new law of life is fulfilled in us by Christ (not by us) as we walk after the Spirit. Through Him we're accounted righteous.

v.5 The main concerns of the flesh are: What shall we eat? What shall we drink? What shall we wear?

v.6 The mind of the flesh is death; the mind of the Spirit is life and peace. As we allow the Spirit to govern our minds, we think in conformity to the will of God.

v.7-8 The flesh is in rebellion to God's laws, so we cannot please God as long as we're in the flesh.

v.9 We're not in the flesh when we allow God's Spirit to dwell in us.

v.11 The Holy Spirit brings us into the resurrected life of Christ.

v.12 We don't owe the flesh anything!

v.13 Through the power of the Spirit, we're enabled to put to death the deeds of the flesh.

v.15 "Abba" means "father."

v.17 Matthew 25:34.

v.18 II Corinthians 4:17.

v.19 All of creation waits expectantly for the redemption of our bodies when we'll finally be in a body that is in harmony with our spirit.

v.20 "Vanity" means "emptiness."

v.23 "They" refers to the world around us.

v.24-25 Our hope is for that new body from God.

v.26-27 "Infirmities" means "weaknesses." The purpose of prayer is never to get our will done, but to get God's will done. It's a waste of time to pray for things that are contrary to God's will. Sometimes, we don't know God's will in a certain situation; then the Holy Spirit interprets our groanings and intercedes with God for us, according to God's will.

v.28 This beautiful verse sustains us in times of painful trials.

v.29 God predestined those He knew would respond to His love and grace. When God watches our lives, it's as if He were watching a rerun, because He knows what we will do (Psalm 90:9). Christ was the first-born.

v.30-31 God chose us, called us, justified us, and glorified us. He is for us. The world, the flesh, and the devil are against us, but they're no match for God.

v.33 Satan accuses us, but God justifies us.

v.34 The difference between Satan's condemnation and the Holy Spirit's conviction is that the condemnation makes us want to pull away from God, because we feel unworthy; while the conviction makes us want to go to God to make things right. Jesus doesn't want to condemn us. He pleads our case for us.

ROMANS 9: CHOSEN

v.1-3 Paul continually sorrowed that the Jews didn't accept Jesus as the Messiah.

v.4 God adopted the children of Israel as His special people. The glory of God's presence filled the tabernacle and the temple. God made a covenant with the people that He would be their God and they would be His people. God gave the Law and the order for service to Him (Leviticus). God gave numerous promises to Israel, some that are still in effect today.

v.5 The great patriarchs belonged to Israel.

This text should read "...Christ came, who is God over all, blessed forever." Jesus is God (Titus 2:13).

v.6-9 Paul here demonstrates that not all of the children of Israel were acknowledged by God as His people.

v.10-13 God had chosen Jacob, because He knew that Jacob would be a spiritual man and Esau would be a fleshly man.

v.14 The choices God has made haven't closed the door to one individual. He loves and accepts all who come to Him.

v.15-18 Since God is supreme, He can choose and act as He pleases. His ways are beyond our human understanding.

v.24 God has called us (the Church) out from among the Jews and Gentiles that He might display His mercy through us.

v.27 Only a remnant of Israel will be saved, so being Jewish doesn't guarantee salvation.

v.30 The Gentiles, who didn't follow the Law, gained righteousness through faith.

v.31-33 Jesus was the stumbling stone. The idea of righteousness by faith was difficult for the Jews to accept after the years they'd spent seeking righteousness by the Law.

ROMANS 10: SAVED

v.1-3 Paul wasn't bitter against the Jews for fighting his attempts to bring Christ to them. He was longing to release them from their futile attempts to become righteous by following the Law.

v.4 Christ brings an end to the Law for those who believe.

v.5 The righteousness of the Law is based on man's doing; the righteousness of faith is based on the work Christ has done.

v.8-10 We only have to speak the words of faith in Jesus to attain all His righteousness.

v.11-13 God delights to show mercy and will not turn away any who come to Him. He doesn't take more pleasure in a Jew coming to salvation than a Gentile.

v.14-15 This passage contains the reason we send missionaries out.

v.17 This "word" refers to the spoken word.

v.18 Psalm 19:4. Nature testifies to God's existence.

ROMANS 11: NATURAL AND SPIRITUAL ISRAEL

v.1-4 God hasn't cast off Israel. He defended them when Elijah complained to Him.

v.5 God has a remnant among the Jews today who believe in Jesus as their Messiah.

v.6 We're accepted by God either by our works or by grace; it cannot be both.

v.7-8 God has blinded those who reject His grace.

v.11 Through the cutting off of the Jews, an opening was made for the Gentiles.

v.12 When God restores the Jews to His favor, the Kingdom Age will begin.

v.17 The Gentiles are the wild olive tree grafted into the good olive tree of the Jews, with the blessings of the covenant and the promises.

v.20-21 God grafted us by our faith in Christ. The Jews were cut off because of their unbelief, not merely to make room for us.

v.25 The "fulness of the Gentiles" indicates that there are a number of Gentiles who will be saved, after which God will turn back to Israel, drawing His people unto Himself.

v.28 God calls the Jews His "elect" (Matthew 24).

v.32 The Jews are now in unbelief of God, so that He can extend His mercy to them.

v.33 God doesn't ask us to reconcile the various truths about

His relations with man. He only wants us to believe, trusting Him with simple faith.

v.36 Everything is centered around God.

ROMANS 12: THE LIVING SACRIFICE

v.1 "Reasonable" means "logical." It makes sense to let God direct our lives.

v.2 God leads us in very natural ways when we make ourselves available to Him.

v.3 I Corinthians 4:7; Ephesians 2:8, 9.

v.6 God gives us a gift suitable for our ministry in the body.

v.8 The exhorter gives us a little shove in the right direction.

v.9 Show love without partiality; love all equally.

v.10-21 These verses are exhortations from Paul on the way we should live as Christians.

v.20 Heaping coals of fire on someone's head refers to the fact that people often carried coals in packs on their backs and were given live coals by friends. It was a gracious act.

ROMANS 13: OBEDIENCE AND LOVE

v.1 Sometimes God ordains an evil ruler, because He plans to bring judgment on a country.

v.3-4 People who obey the law need not fear the police. They're here to protect us, and we should have an appreciative attitude toward them.

v.6-7 "Tribute" means "taxes."

v.8-10 Love for one another sums up the Law and makes it a positive command, rather than a list of negatives.

v.13 This verse names the works of darkness we're to cast off.

v.14 This verse tells us that the armor of light is Jesus Christ.

ROMANS 14: JUDGING OTHERS

v.1 We shouldn't judge those who are weak in faith but accept them with love.

v.2-3 Paul here talks of vegetarians who were weak in the faith because they felt convicted about eating meat.

v.5-6 Others who were weak in the faith felt that there were certain days when the Lord should be worshiped.

v.7 Paul encouraged the Christians to allow each other their personal convictions without trying to put them on every one else.

v.10 To "set at nought" a brother is to say that he isn't a Christian.

v.11-12 When we stand before God for judgment, it won't be to determine our salvation, for that is already secure. He'll judge our works and the motivation behind our works, then give us our place in His kingdom (Philippians 2:10, 11).

v.13-15 Paul here warns against enjoying our freedom in Christ to the detriment of our weaker fellow-Christians.

v.18 God accepts us and men approve us if we're walking in the Spirit.

v.20 We shouldn't destroy the work of God in a person's life because we disagree about eating meat. We can do something that isn't wrong in itself but is evil because it offends someone else.

v.22-23 It's wrong to try to argue someone out of his convictions, because his conscience will condemn him if he does something he believes is a sin.

ROMANS 15: CHRISTIAN UNITY

v.1 We that are strong in the faith should be helping the weaker brothers to stand.

v.3 Christ took reproaches on Himself that were aimed at God, because He didn't live to please Himself.

v.5-7 We should seek unity in the body, accepting one another.

v.8 Jesus ministered to the Jews, the "circumcision," because He came to fulfill God's promises to the Jews.

v.9-12 Paul gives the Scriptures that prophesied the inclusion of the Gentiles in God's grace.

v.13 Paul here begins an extended benediction and series of prayers to close the epistle.

v.16-19 Paul says his ministry to the Gentiles was proper because the Holy Spirit ordained it.

v.22-24 Paul hadn't visited the church in Rome before.

v.26 The saints in Jerusalem were poor, because they had sold their possessions to share everything in common.

v.30 Paul asked the Christians to strive and persevere in their prayers for him—important words relating to prayer.

v.31-32 Paul asked them to pray for three things: (I) that he be delivered from the unbelievers in Judea, (2) that the offering would be accepted by the Jerusalem church, (3) that he could visit Rome with joy and be refreshed.

ROMANS 16: BLESSINGS

v.1-2 "Servant" here means "deaconess." Phoebe carried this epistle from Paul to Rome.

v.3-5 Paul met Priscilla and Aquila when he first went to Corinth. Wherever they lived, they opened their home for Bible studies and helped to establish new believers.

v.7 Junia is a feminine name. Apparently, there were women apostles.

v.17-18 Differences over doctrinal matters were too dangerous to overlook. Paul warns the Christians to take note of those who brought divisions into the Church and to avoid them.

v.19 Their obedience to Christ was well-known.

Paul wanted the Christians to be wise in spiritual things but unlearned in evil things.

v.20 Genesis 3 :15 .

v.25 "Mystery" refers to something now revealed that had previously been unknown, not something that couldn't be known.